GOD SAID....

A message from Heaven

Hazel Harris

WESTBOW
PRESS®
A DIVISION OF THOMAS NELSON
& ZONDERVAN

WestBow Press books may be ordered through booksellers or by contacting:

WestBow Press
A Division of Thomas Nelson & Zondervan
1663 Liberty Drive
Bloomington, IN 47403
www.westbowpress.com
844-714-3454

Scripture taken from the King James Version of the Bible.
A KJV Regency Bible, Thomas Nelson Publishers Copyright 1990

ISBN: 978-1-6642-5385-8 (sc)
ISBN: 978-1-6642-5384-1 (e)

Print information available on the last page.

WestBow Press rev. date: 01/14/2021

THE ART OF CROSS REFERENCING

This Word came out of my prayer closet in the year 2014. The Lord showed me how to assemble this masterpiece.

After I read the message in its entirety, I learned a great more deal about the way God uses His Word to speak.

This message became the most interesting read I have ever experienced. As I read through in the order it was given, I heard the LORD God speaking and wanted to share this with everyone.

In these end times, hearing from God was what I needed most.

(Isaiah 54:13) And all thy children shall be taught of the LORD; and great shall be the peace of thy children.

Cross referencing became a great way of covering Scripture in both Old and New Testament.

I noticed that the LORD God was always speaking and if I removed the chapter and verse, I wouldn't be able to tell Old from New. It just became a conversation.

After finishing this manuscript, I continued the process. I would pick a topic and cross reference. This became a daily practice because I noticed that having my Bible open each day was like a protective shield. I never ran out of topics of interest.

Now I understand why the enemy of God does not want us to own a Bible or to open our Bibles. The Word of God quenches the thirst of our souls. He gives us direction, instruction and answers to life's toughest problems. He heals and restores. He speaks to us through His Word, but only if we are paying Him attention.

A message revealed from Heaven

TIMELINE: ABOUT 1446 AND 1406 B.

God said...

*Genesis 3:15 "And **I** will put enmity between thee and the woman, and between thy seed and her **Seed. He** shall bruise thy head, and thou shalt bruise **His** heel"

*Genesis 12:2 "And **I** will make of thee a great nation, and **I** will bless thee, and make thy name great; and thou shalt be a blessing".

Galatians 3:8 "And the Scriptures, forseeing that **God** would justify the heathen through faith, preached before the gospel unto Abraham, saying, "In thee shall all nations be blessed"

*Genesis 17:7 And **I** will establish **My** Covenant between **Me** and thee and thy seed after thee in their generations for an everlasting Covenant, to be a **God** unto thee, and to thy seed after thee.

*Genesis 22:18 And in thy seed shall all the nations of the Earth be blessed because thou hast obeyed **My** voice.

*Genesis 26:4 **I** will make thy seed to multiply as the stars of Heaven and will give unto thy seed all these countries; and in thy seed shall all the nations of the Earth be blessed.

Galatians 3:8 and the Scriptures, forseeing that **God** would justify the heathen through faith, preached before the gospel unto Abraham, saying, in thee shall all nations be blessed.

God said....

Genesis 49:10 The Scepter shall not depart from Judah, nor a lawgiver from between his feet, until **Shiloh** come; and unto **Him** shall the gathering of the people be.

Psalm 60:7 Gilead is **Mine**, and Manasseh is **Mine**; Ephraim also is the strength of **Mine** head; Judah is **My** lawgiver;

Revelation 5:5 And one of the elders saith unto me, weep not: behold, the **Lion** of the tribe of Judah, the **Root** of David, hath prevailed to open the book, and to loose the seven seals thereof.

Numbers 9:12 They shall leave none of it unto the morning, nor break any bone of it: according to all the ordinances of the Passover they shall keep it.

Exodus 12:10 And ye shall let nothing of it remain until the morning; and that which remaineth of it until the morning ye shall burn with fire.

John 19:36 For these things were done that the Scriptures should be fulfilled, "Not one of **His** bones shall be broken"

Numbers 24:17 I shall see **Him**, but not now: I shall behold **Him**, but not nigh: there shall come a **Star** out of Jacob, and a **Sceptre** shall rise out of Israel, and shall smite the corners of Moab, and destroy all the children of Sheth.

Deuteronomy 18:15 The **LORD** thy **God** will raise up unto thee a **Prophet** from the midst of thee, of thy brethren, like unto me; unto **Him** ye shall hearken;

John 1:45 Philip findeth Nathanael, and saith unto him, we have found **Him** of whom Moses in the law, and the prophets did write, **Jesus** of Nazareth, the **Son** of Joseph.

Deuteronomy 32:43 Rejoice, O ye nations, with **His** people: for **He** will avenge the blood of **His** servants, and will render vengeance to **His** adversaries, and will be merciful unto **His** land, and to **His** people.

Romans 15:10 and again he saith, REJOICE, YE GENTILES, WITH **HIS** PEOPLE.

Revelations 19:2 for True and Righteous are **His** judgments: for **He** hath judged the great whore, which did corrupt the Earth with her fornication, and hath avenged the blood of **His** servants at her hand.

Psalm 85:1 **LORD, Thou** hast been favourable unto **Thy** land: **Thou** hast brought back the captivity of Jacob.

TIMELINE: 1ST AND 2ND REIGN OF SAMUEL ABOUT 970 TO 930 B.C.

*2 Samuel 7:13 **He** shall build a House for **My** Name, and **I** will stablish the Throne of **His** Kingdom forever.

Matthew 19:28 And **Jesus** said unto them, "Verily **I** say unto you, that ye which have followed **Me**, in the regeneration when the **Son** of Man shall sit in the Throne of **His** Glory, ye also shall sit upon twelve thrones, judging the twelve tribes of Israel".

*2 Samuel 22:3 The **God** of my **Rock**; in **Him** will I trust: **He** is my **Shield** and the **Horn** of my Salvation, my **High Tower**, and my **Refuge**, my **Savior**; **Thou** savest me from violence.

*Job 19:25 For I know that my **Redeemer** liveth, and that **He** shall stand at the latter day upon the Earth:

Psalm 78:35 And they remembered that **God** was their **Rock** and the **Most High God** their **Redeemer**.

TIMELINE: PERHAPS, 950 B.C.

*Psalm 2:1 Why do the heathen rage, and the people imagine a vain thing?

Acts 4:25-28 Who by the mouth of **Thy** servant David hast said, "WHY DID THE HEATHEN RAGE AND THE

PEOPLE IMAGINE VAIN THINGS?" 26) THE KINGS OF THE EARTH STOOD UP, AND THE RULERS WERE

GATHERED TOGETHER AGAINST THE **LORD** AND AGAINST **HIS CHRIST** 27) For of a truth against **Thy Holy Child Jesus,** whom **Thou** hast anointed, both Herod, and Pontius Pilate, with the Gentiles, and the people of Israel, were gathered together. 28) for to do whatsoever **Thy** hand and **Thy** counsel determined before to be done.

*Psalm 2:7 **I** will declare the decree: the **LORD** hath said unto **Me.** "**Thou** art **My Son**; this day have **I Begotten Thee.**

*Psalm 2:9 **Thou** shalt break them with an rod of iron; **Thou** shalt dash them in pieces like a potter's vessel.

Psalm 110:5, 6 The **LORD** at **Thy** right hand shall strike trough kings in the day of **His** wrath. 6) **He** shall judge among the heathen; **He** shall fill the places with the dead bodies; **He** shall wound the heads over many countries.

God said....

Psalm 8:2 Out of the mouth of babes and sucklings hast **Thou** ordained strength because of **Thine** enemies, that **Thou** mightiest still the enemy and the avenger.

Matthew 21:15, 16 And when the chief priest and scribes say the wonderful things that **He** did, and the children crying in the Temple, saying, "Hosanna to the **Son** of David"; they were sore displeased, 16) and

saith unto **Him**, "Hearst **Thou** what these say?" And **Jesus** saith unto them, "Yea; have ye never read, OUT OF THE MOUTH OF BABES AND SUCKLINGS **THOU** HAS PERFECTED PRAISE?"

Psalm 16:10 For **Thou** wilt not leave **My Soul** in hell; neither wilt **Thou** suffer **Thine Holy One** to see corruption.

Psalm 22:1 "**My God, My God**, why hast **Thou** forsaken **Me**? Why art **Thou** so far from helping **Me**, and from the words of **My** roaring?"

Mark 15:34 And at the ninth hour, **Jesus** cried with a loud voice, saying, "**Eloi, Eloi, Lama Sabachthani**?", which is being interpreted, "**My God, My God**, why hast **Thou** forsaken **Me**"?

Psalm 22:7 All they that see **Me** laugh **Me** to scorn: they shoot out the lip, they shake the head,

Matthew 27:39 And they that passed by reviled **Him**, wagging their heads.

Psalm 22:8 Saying, "**He** trusted on the **LORD** that **He** would deliver **Him**: let **Him** deliver **Him**, seeing **He** delighted in **Him**".

Psalm 22:16 For dogs have compassed **Me**: the assembly of the wicked have enclosed **Me**: they pierced **My** hands and **My** feet.

John 20:27 Then saith **He** to Thomas, "Reach hither thy finger, and behold **My** hands; and reach hither thy hand and thrust it into **My** side: and be not faithless but believing".

*Psalm 22:17 **I** may tell all **My** bones: they look and stare upon **Me**.

John 19:37 And again another Scripture saith, "They shall look on **Him**, whom they pierced".

*Psalm 22:18 They part **My** garments among them and cast lots upon **My** vesture.

Luke 23:34 Then **Jesus** said, "**Father**, forgive them, for they do not know what they do." And they divided **His** garments and cast lots.

*Psalm 22:22 **I** will declare **Thy** Name unto **My** brethren: in the midst of the congregation will **I** praise **Thee**.

*Psalm 27:12 Deliver **Me** not over unto the will of **Mine** enemies: for false witnesses are risen up against **Me**, as such as breathe out cruelty.

*Psalm 34:20 **He** keepeth all **His** bones: not one of them is broken.

John 19:33 But when they came to **Jesus**, and saw that **He** was dead already, they brake not **His** legs:

John 19:36 For these things were done, that the Scripture should be fulfilled, "A bone of **Him** shall not be broken".

*Psalm 35:11 False witnesses did rise up; they laid to My charge things that **I** knew not.

Mark 14:57 And there arose certain, and bare false witnesses against **Him**,

*Psalm 35:19 Let not them that are **Mine** enemies wrongfully rejoice over **Me**: neither let them wink with the eye that hate **Me** without a cause.

Proverbs 6:13 He winketh with his eyes, he speaketh with his feet, he teacheth with his fingers.

God said....

Psalm 41:9 Yea, **Mine** own familiar friend, in whom **I** trusted, which did eat of **My** bread, hath lifted up his heel against **Me.**

John 13:18 **I** speak not of you all: **I** know whom **I** have chosen but that the Scripture may be fulfilled, HE THAT EATETH BREAD WITH **ME** HATH LIFTED UP HIS HEEL AGAINST **ME.**

John 17:12 While **I** was with them in the world, **I** kept them in **Thy** Name: those that **Thou** gavest **Me**, **I** have kept, and none of them is lost, but the son of perdition; that the Scripture might be fulfilled.

Psalm 45:6 "**Thy** Throne, **O God**, is for ever and ever: the Sceptre of **Thy** Kingdom is a right Sceptre".

Psalm 93:2 "**Thy** Throne is established of old: **Thou** art from everlasting".

Hebrew 1:8, 9 But unto the **Son, He** saith, "**Thy** Throne, **O God**, is for ever and ever: a Sceptre of Righteousness is the Sceptre of **Thy** Kingdom". "**Thou** hast loved Righteousness, and hated iniquity; therefore **God**, even **Thy God**, hath anointed **Thee** with the Oil of Gladness above **Thy** fellows".

Psalm 49:15 "But **God** will redeem **My Soul** from the power of the grave: for **He** shall receive **Me**".

Psalm 68:18 "**Thou** hast ascended on High, **Thou** hast let captivity captive: **Thou** hast received gifts for men; yea, for the rebellious also, that the **LORD God** might dwell among them.

Psalm 69:4 "They that hate **Me** without a cause are more than the hairs of **Mine** head: they that would destroy **Me**, being **Mine** enemies wrongfully are might: then **I** restored that which **I** took not away".

John 15:25 But this cometh to pass, that the Word might be fulfilled that is written in their law, "They hated **Me** without a cause".

Psalm 69:9 "For the zeal of **Thine** house hath eaten **Me** up; and the reproaches of them that reproached **Thee** are fallen upon **Me**"

*Psalm 69:21 "They gave **Me** also gall for **My** meat; and in **My** thirst they gave **Me** vinegar to drink".

Matthew 27:34 They gave **Him** vinegar to drink mingled with gall: and when **He** had tasted thereof, **He** would not drink. Matthew 27:48 And straightway one of them ran and took a spunge, and filled it with vinegar, and put it on a reed, and gave **Him** to drink.

*Psalm 72:4 **He** shall judge the poor of the people, **He** shall save the children of the needy, and shall break in pieces the oppressor.

Isaiah 11:4 But with Righteousness shall **He** judge the poor and reprove with equity for the meek of the Earth: and **He** shall smite the Earth with the rod of **His** mouth, and with the breath of **His** lips shall **He** slay the wicked.

*Psalm 72:5 They shall fear **Thee** as long as the sun and moon endure, throughout all generations.

Psalm 89:36, 37 **His Seed** shall endure forever, and **His** Throne as the sun before **Me**. 37) It shall be established forever, as the moon, and as a faithful witness in Heaven.

Isaiah 9:7 Of the increase of **His** Government and Peace there shall be no end, upon the Throne of David, and upon **His** Kingdom, to order it, and to establish it with judgment and with justice from henceforth even forever. The zeal of the **LORD** of Hosts will perform this.

*Psalm 72:9 They that dwell in the wilderness shall bow before **Him**; and **His** enemies shall lick the dust.

Isaiah 49:23 And kings shall be thy nursing fathers, and their queens thy nursing mothers: they shall bow down to thee with their face toward the Earth, and lick up the dust of thy feet; and thou shalt know that **I** am the **LORD**: for they shall not be ashamed that wait for **Me**.

God said....

Psalm 72:11 Yea, all kings shall fall down before **Him**: all nations shall serve **Him**.

Isaiah 49:23 And kings shall be thy nursing fathers, and their queens thy nursing mothers: they shall bow down to thee with their faces toward the Earth, and lick up the dust of thy feet; and thou shalt know that **I** am the **LORD**: for they shall not be ashamed that wait for **Me**.

Psalm 72:17 **His** Name shall endure forever: **His** Name shall be continued as long as the sun: and men shall be blessed in **Him**: all nations shall call **Him** Blessed.

Psalm 89:36 **His** Seed shall endure forever, and **His** Throne as the sun before **Me**.

Psalm 78:2 **I** will open my mouth in a parable: I will utter dark sayings of old:

Psalm 44:1 We have heard with our ears, **O God**, our fathers have told us what work **Thou** didst in their days, in the times of old.

Psalm 102:25 Of old hast **Thou** laid the foundation of the Earth: and the Heavens are the work of **Thy** hands.

Genesis 1:1 In the beginning **God** created the Heaven and the Earth.

Psalm 109:4 For my love they are my adversaries: but I give myself unto prayer.

Psalm 110:4 The **LORD** hath sworn, and will not repent, "**Thou** art a Priest forever after the Order of Melchizedek".

Psalm 118:26 Blessed be he that cometh in the Name of the **LORD**: we have blessed you out of the House of the **Lord**.

TIMELINE: ISAIAH'S MINISTRY FROM ABOUT 740 TO 680 B.C.

*Isaiah 2:2, 3 And it shall come to pass in the last days, that the mountains of the **LORD's** House shall be established in the top of the mountains and shall be exalted above the hills; and all nations shall flow unto it. 3) And many people shall go and say, "Come ye, and let us go up to the Mountain of the **LORD**, to the House of the **God** of Jacob; and **He** will teach us of **His** ways, and we will walk in **His** paths: for out of Zion shall go forth the law, and the Word of the **LORD** from Jerusalem".

Jeremiah 50:5 They shall ask the way to Zion with their faces thitherward, saying, "Come, and let us join ourselves to the **LORD** in a perpetual Covenant that shall not be forgotten".

*Isaiah 6:9 And **He** said, "Go, and tell this people, 'Hear ye indeed, but understand not; and see ye indeed, but perceive not'".

Matthew 13:14, 15 And in them is fulfilled the prophecy of Esaias, which saith, "BY HEARING YE SHALL

HEAR, AND SHALL NOT UNDRESTAND; AND SEEING YE SHALL SEE AND SHALL NOT PERCEIVE: FOR THIS

PEOPLE'S HEART IS WAXED GROSS, AND THEIR EARS ARE DULL OF HEARING, AND THEIR EYES HAVE CLOSED; LEST AT ANY TIME THEY SHOULD SEE WITH THEIR EYES, AND

God said....

HEAR WITH THEIR HEART, AND SHOULD BE CONVERTED,". AND **I** SHOULD HEAL THEM.

Isaiah 6:10 Make the heart of this people fat, and make their ears heavy, and shut their eyes; lest they see with their eyes, and hear with their ears, and understand with their heart, and convert, and be healed.

Mark 6:1-6 And **He** went out from thence and came into **His** own country; and **His** disciples followed

Him. 2) And when the Sabbath day was come, **He** began to teach in the synagogue: and many hearing **Him** were astonished, saying, "From whence hath this **Man** these things: and what wisdom is this which is given unto **Him**, that even such might works are wrought by **His** hands? 3) Is not this the **Carpenter**, the **Son** of Mary, the brother of James, and Joses, and of Juda, and Simon? And are not **His** sisters here with us? And they were offended at **Him**. 4) But **Jesus** said unto them, "A prophet is not without honour, but in his own country, and among his own kin, and in his own house". 5) And **He** could there do no mighty work, save that **He** laid **His** hands upon a few sick folks and healed them. 6) And **He** marveled because of their unbelief. And **He** went round about the villages, teaching.

Isaiah 7:14 Therefore, the **LORD Himself,** shall give you a sign; Behold, a virgin shall conceive, and bear a **Son**, and shall call **His** Name **Immanuel**.

Isaiah 8:14 And **He** shall be for a Sanctuary, but for a Stone of Stumbling and for a Rock of Offence to both the Houses of Israel, for a gin and for a snare to the inhabitants of Jerusalem.

Isaiah 8:18 Behold, **I** and the children whom the **LORD** hath given **Me** are for the signs and for wonders in Israel from the **LORD** of Hosts, which dwelleth in Mount Zion.

Hebrew 2:13 And again, **I** will put **My** trust in **Him**, and again, Behold **I** and the children which **God** hath given **Me**.

*Isaiah 9:1 Nevertheless the dimness shall not be such as was in her vexation, when at the first **He** lightly afflicted the land of Zebulun and the land of Naphtali, and afterward did more grievously afflict her by the way of the sea, beyond Jordan, in Galilee of the nations.

Matthew 4:14-16 That it might be fulfilled which was spoken by Esaias the prophet, saying 15) "THE LAND OF ZABULON, AND THE LAND OF NEPHTHALIM, BY THE WAY OF THE SEA, BEYOND

JORDAN, GALILEE OF THE GENTILES; 16) THE PEOPLE WHICH SAT IN DARKNESS SAW GREAT **LIGHT**; AND TO THEM WHICH SAT IN THE REGION AND SHADOW OF DEATH, **LIGHT** IS SPUNG UP".

*Isaiah 9:2 The people that walked in darkness have seen a great **Light**: they that dwell in the land of the shadow of death, upon them hath the **Light** shined.

Luke 1:79 To give **Light** to them that sit in darkness and in the shadow of death, to guide our feet into the way of Peace.

*Isaiah 9:6 For unto us a child is born, unto us a **Son** is given: and the Government shall be upon **His** shoulders: and **His** Name shall be called **Wonderful**, **Counselor**, The **Mighty God**, The **Everlasting Father**, The **Prince of Peace**.

Isaiah 7:14 Therefore the **Lord Himself,** shall give you a sign; "Behold, a virgin shall conceive, and bear a **Son**, and shall call **His** Name **Immanuel**".

Luke 2:11 for unto you is born this day in the city of David a **Saviour**, which is **Christ** the **Lord**.

Titus 2:13 Looking for that blessed hope, and the glorious appearing of the great **God** and our **Saviour Jesus Christ**.

TIMELINE: 701 TO 681 B.C.

*Isaiah 9:7 Of the increase of **His** Government and Peace there shall be no end, upon the Throne of David, and upon **His** Kingdom, to order it, and to establish it with judgement and with justice from henceforth even forever. The Zeal of the **LORD** of Hosts will perform this.

*Isaiah 11:1, 2 And there shall come forth a **Rod** out of the stem of Jesse, and a **Branch** shall grow out of his roots: 2) And the **Spirit** of the **LORD** shall rest upon **Him**, The **Spirit** of Wisdom and Understanding, The **Spirit** of Counsel and Might, The **Spirit** of Knowledge and the Fear of the **LORD**;

Isaiah 42:1 Behold, **My Servant, Whom I** uphold; **Mine Elect**, in **Whom My Soul** delighteth; **I** have put **My Spirit** upon **Him**; **He** shall bring forth judgment to the Gentiles.

*Isaiah 11:10 And in that day there shall be a **Root** of Jesse, which shall stand for an ensign of the people; to whom shall the Gentiles seek; and **His** rest shall be glorious.

*Isaiah 22:22 And the Key of the House of David will lay upon **His** shoulders; so **He** shall open, and none shall shut; and **He** shall shut, and none shall open.

Revelation 3:7 And to the angel of the church in Philadelphia, write; These things saith **He** that is **Holy**, **He** that is True, **He** that hath the Key of David, **He** that openeth, and no man shutteth; and shutteth, and no man openeth;

God said....

Job 12:14 Behold, **He** breaketh down, and it cannot be built again: **He** shutteth up a man, and there can be no opening.

Isaiah 28:16 Therefore, thus saith the **LORD GOD**, "Behold, **I** lay in Zion for a **Foundation**, a **Stone**, a **Tried Stone**, a **Precious Corner Stone**, a **Sure Foundation**: he that believeth shall not make haste".

1 Peter 2:6-8 Wherefore also it is contained in the Scripture, "Behold **I** lay in Sion a **Chief Corner Stone, Elect, Precious**: and he that believeth on **Him** shall not be confounded. 7) Unto you therefore which believe **He** is **Precious**: but unto them which be disobedient, the **Stone** which the builders disallowed, the same is made the **Head** of the **Corner** 8) and a **Stone** of **Stumbling**, and a **Rock** of **Offence**, even to them which stumble at the **Word**, being disobedient: whereunto also they were appointed".

Isaiah 29:13 Wherefore the **LORD** said, "Forasmuch, as this people draw near to **Me** with their mouth, and with their lips do honour **Me**, but have removed their heart far from **Me**, and their fear toward **Me** is taught by the precept of men:"

Ezekiel 33:31 And they come unto **Thee** as the people cometh, and they sit before **Thee** as **My** people, and they hear **Thy** words, but they will not do them: for with their mouth they shew much love, but their heart goeth after their covetousness:

Mark 7:6, 7 **He** answered, and said unto them, "Well hath Esaias prophesied of you hypocrites, as it is written, 'This people honoureth **Me** with their lips, but their heart is far from **Me**'.

Isaiah 29:13 Wherefore the **LORD** said, Forsomuch as the people draw near **Me** with their mouth, and with their lips do honour **Me**, but have removed their heart far from **Me**, and their fear toward **Me** is taught by the precept of men:

Mark 7:7 "Howbeit in vain do they worship **Me**, teaching for doctrines, the commandments of men".

✻Isaiah 35:5 Then the eyes of the blind shall be opened, and the ears of the deaf shall be unstopped.

John 9:6, 7 When **He** had thus spoken, **He** spat on the ground, and made clay of the spittle, and **He** anointed the eyes of the blind man with the clay, 7) And said unto him, "Go, wash in the pool of Siloam", (which is by interpretation, Sent)". He went his way therefore, and washed, and came seeing.

✻Isaiah 40:3 The voice of him that crieth in the wilderness, "Prepare ye the way of the **LORD**, make straight in the desert a highway for our **God**"?

Matthew 3:3 For this is **He** that was spoken of by the prophet Esaias, saying, "The voice of one crying in the wilderness, prepare ye the way of the **LORD**, make **His** paths straight".

✻Isaiah 40:11 **He** shall feed **His** flock like a shepherd: **He** shall gather the lambs with **His** arm and carry them in **His** bosom and shall gently lead those that are with young.

Micah 5:4 and **He** shall stand and feed in the strength of the **LORD**, in the **Majesty** of the **Name** of the **LORD His God**; and they shall abide: for now shall **He** be Great unto the ends of the Earth.

✻Isaiah 42:1 Behold **My Servant**, **Whom I** uphold; **Mine Elect**, in **Whom My Soul** delighteth; **I** have put **My Spirit** upon **Him**: **He** shall bring forth judgment to the Gentiles.

Luke 3:22 And the **Holy Ghost** descended in a bodily shape like a dove upon **Him**, and a **Voice** came from Heaven, which said, "**Thou** art **My Beloved Son**; in **Thee I** am well pleased".

✻Isaiah 42:4 **He** shall not fail nor be discouraged, till **He** have set judgment in the Earth: and the isles shall wait for **His** law.

God said....

Genesis 49:10 the Scepter shall not depart from Judah, nor a lawgiver from between his feet, until **Shiloh** come; and unto **Him** shall the gathering of the people be.

Isaiah 42:7 To open the blind eyes, to bring out the prisoners from the prison, and them that sit in darkness out of the prison house.

Isaiah 35:5 Then the eyes of the blind shall be opened, and the ears of the deaf shall be unstopped.

Isaiah 45:23 **I** have sworn by **Myself**, the **Word** is gone out of **My** mouth in Righteousness and shall not return. That unto **Me** every knee shall bow, every tongue shall swear.

Isaiah 49:2 And **He** hath made **My** mouth like a sharp sword; in the shadow of **His** hand hath **He** hid **Me**, and made **Me** a polished shaft; in **His** quiver hath **He** hid **Me**;

Isaiah 11:4 But with Righteousness shall **He** judge the poor and reprove with equity for the meek of the Earth: and **He** shall smite the Earth with the Rod of **His** mouth, and with the breath of **His** lips shall **He** slay the wicked.

Revelations 1:16 And **He** had in **His** right hand seven stars: and out of **His** mouth went a sharp two-edged sword: and **His** countenance was as the sun shineth in **His** strength.

Revelations 2:12 And the angel of the church in Pergamos write; These things saith **He** which hath the sharp sword with two edges.

Isaiah 49:5 And now, saith the **LORD** that formed **Me** from the womb to be **His Servant**, to bring Jacob again to **Him**, Though Israel be not gathered, yet shall **I** be Glorious in the eyes of the **LORD**, and **My God** shall be **My** strength.

Matthew 23:37 O Jerusalem, Jerusalem, thou that killest the prophets, and stonest them which are sent unto thee, how often would **I** have to gathered they children together, even as a hen gathereth her chickens under her wings and ye would not!

Isaiah 43:4 Since thou wast precious in **My** sight, thou hast been honourable and have loved thee: therefore, will **I** give men for thee, and people for thy life.

Isaiah 12:2 Behold, **God** is my Salvation; I will trust, and not be afraid: for the **LORD JEHOVAH** is my strength and my song; **He** also is become my Salvation.

✲Isaiah 49:6 And **He** said, "It is a light thing that **Thou** shouldest be **My Servant** to raise up the tribes of Jacob, and to restore the preserved of Israel: **I** will also give **Thee** for a **Light** to the Gentiles, that **Thou** mayest be **My** Salvation unto the end of the Earth.

Luke 2:32 A **Light** to lighten the Gentiles, and the Glory of **Thy** people Israel.

✲Isaiah 49:7 Thus saith the **LORD**, the **Redeemer** of Israel, and **His Holy One,** to **Him** whom man despiseth, to **Him** whom the nation abhoreth, to a **Servant** of rulers: Kings shall see and arise, princes also shall worship, because of the **LORD** that is faithful, and the **Holy One** of Israel, and **He** shall choose **Thee**.

Psalm 22:6-8 But **I** am a worm, and no man; a reproach of men, and despised of the people. 7)

All they that see **Me** laugh **Me** to scorn: they shoot out the lip, they shake the head, saying, 8) "**He** trusted on the **LORD** that **He** would deliver **Him**: let **Him** deliver **Him**, seeing **He** delighted in **Him**.

✲Isaiah 49:8 Thus saith the **Lord**, "In an acceptable time have **I** heard **Thee**, and in a day of Salvation have **I** helped **Thee**: and **I** will preserve **Thee**, and give **Thee** for a Covenant of the people, to establish the Earth, to cause to inherit the desolate heritages.

God said....

2 Corinthians 6:2 (For **He** saith, **I** have heard thee in a time accepted, and in the day of Salvation have **I** succoured thee: Behold, now is the excepted time; Behold, now is the day of Salvation.)

Isaiah 49:9 That **Thou** mayest say to the prisoners, "Go forth; to them that are in darkness, shew yourselves". They shall feed in the ways, and their pastures shall be in all high places.

Isaiah 49:10 They shall not hunger not thirst; neither shall the heat nor sun smite them: for **He** that hath mercy on them shall lead them, even by the springs of water shall **He** guide them.

Isaiah 50:5 The **LORD GOD** hath opened **Mine** ear, **I** was not rebellious, neither turned away back.

Psalm 40:6-8 Sacrifice and offering **Thou** didst not desire; mine ears hast **Thou** opened: burnt offering and sin offering hast **Thou** not required. 7) Then said I, "Lo, I come in the volume of the book, it is written of me, 8) I delight to do **Thy** will, *O my* **God**: yea, **Thy** law is within my heart.

Isaiah 50:6 **I** gave **My** back to the smiters, and **My** cheeks to them that plucked off the hair: **I** hid not **My** face from shame and spitting.

Matthew 26:67 Then did they spit in **His** face and buffeted **Him**: and others smote **Him** with the palms of their hands.

Isaiah 50:7 For the **LORD GOD** will help **Me**; therefore, shall **I** not be confounded: therefore, have **I** set **My** face like flint, and **I** know that **I** shall not be ashamed.

Luke 9:51 And it came to pass, when the time was come that **He** should be received up, **He** stedfastly set **His** face to go to Jerusalem,

Isaiah 52:14 As many were astonished at **Thee**; **His** visage was so marred more than any man, and **His** form more than the sons of men:

*Isaiah 53:1 **He** shall see of the travail of **His Soul** and shall be satisfied: by **His** knowledge shall **My Righteous Servant** justify many; for **He** shall bear their iniquities.

*Isaiah 53:3 **He** is despised and rejected of men; a **Man** of sorrows and acquainted with grief: and we hid as it were our faces from **Him**: **He** was despised, and we esteemed **Him** not.

John 12:38 That the saying of Esaias the prophet might be fulfilled, which he spake, "**LORD**, who hath believed our report? And to whom hath the arm of the **LORD** been revealed?"

*Isaiah 53:4 Surely, **He** hath borne our griefs, and carried our sorrows: yet we did not esteem **Him** stricken, smitten of **God**, and afflicted.

*Isaiah 53:5 But **He** was wounded for our transgressions, **He** was bruised for our iniquities: the chastisement of our Peace was upon **Him**; and with **His** stripes we are healed.

1 Peter 2:24 **Who His Own Self** bare our sins in **His** own body on the tree that we, being dead to sins, should live unto Righteousness: by **Whose** stripes ye were healed.

*Isaiah 53:7 **He** was oppressed, and **He** was afflicted, yet **He** opened not **His** mouth: **He** is brought as a lamb to the slaughter, and as a sheep before her shearers is dumb, so **He** openeth not **His** mouth.

Matthew 26:63 But **Jesus** held **His** peace. And the high priest answered and said unto **Him**, I adjure **Thee** by the **Living God**, that **Thou** tell us whether **Thou** be the **Christ**, the **Son** of **God**.

Acts 8:32 The place of the Scripture which he read was this, **He** was led as a sheep to the slaughter; and like a lamb dumb before his shearer, so opened **He** not **His** mouth:

God said....

Isaiah 53:9 And **He** made **His** grave with the wicked and with the rich in **His** death; because **He** had done no violence, neither was any deceit in **His** mouth.

Isaiah 53:10 Yet is pleased the **LORD** to bruise **Him**; **He** hath put **Him** to grief: when **Thou** shalt make **His Soul** an offering for sin, **He** shall see **His** seed, **He** shall prolong **His** days, and the pleasure of the **LORD** shall prosper in **His** hand.

John 1:29 The next day John seeth **Jesus** coming unto him, and saith, "Behold the **Lamb** of **God**, which taketh away the sin of the world".

2 Corinthians 5:21 For **He** hath made **Him** to be sin for us, **who** knew no sin; that we might be made the Righteousness of **God** in **Him**.

Isaiah 53:11 **He** shall see the travail of **His Soul** and shall be satisfied: by **His** knowledge shall **My Righteous Servant** justify many; for **He** shall bear their iniquities.

Romans 5:18 Therefore as by the offence of one judgment came upon all men to condemnation; even so by the Righteousness of **One** the free gift came upon all men unto justification of life.

Romans 5:19 For as by one man's disobedience many were made sinners, so by the obedience of **One** shall many be made Righteous.

Isaiah 53:12 Therefore will **I** divide **Him** a portion with the great, and **He** shall divide the spoil with the strong; because **He** hath poured out **His Soul** unto death: and **He** was numbered with the transgressors; and **He** bare the sin of many and made intercession for the transgressors.

Isaiah 50:6 **I** gave **My** back to the smiters, and **My** cheeks to them that plucked off the hair. **I** hid not **My** face from shame and spitting.

Isaiah 54:13 And all thy children shall be taught of the **LORD**; and great shall be the peace of thy children.

Isaiah 11:9 They shall not hurt nor destroy in all **My** Holy Mountain: for the Earth shall be full of the knowledge of the **LORD**, as the waters cover the sea.

*Isaiah 59:20 And the **Redeemer** shall come to Zion, and unto them that turn from transgression in Jacob, saith the **LORD**.

Romans 11:26 And so all Israel shall be saved; as it is written, THERE SHALL COME OUT OF SION THE **DELIVERER**, AND SHALL TURN AWAY UNGODLINESS FROM JACOB:

*Isaiah 61:1 The **Spirit** of the **LORD GOD** is upon **Me**; because the **LORD** hath anointed **Me** to preach good tidings unto the meek; **He** hath sent **Me** to bind up the brokenhearted, to proclaim liberty to the captives, and the opening of the prison to them that are bound.

*Isaiah 62:11 Behold, the **LORD** hath proclaimed unto the end of the world, say ye to the daughter of Zion, "Behold, thy Salvation cometh; behold, **His** reward is with **Him**, and **His** work before **Him**".

Zechariah 9:9 Rejoice greatly, O daughter of Zion; shout, O daughter of Jerusalem: Behold, thy **King** cometh unto thee: **He** is just, and having Salvation; lowly, and riding upon an ass, and upon a colt the foal of an ass.

*Isaiah 63:2 Wherefore art **Thou** red in **Thine** apparel, and **Thy** garments like him that treadeth in the winefat?

*Isaiah 63:3 **I** have trodden the winepress alone; and of the people there was none with **Me**: for **I** will tread them in **Mine** anger and trample them in **My** fury; and their blood shall be sprinkled upon **My** garments and **I** will stain all **My** raiment.

Mark 14:50 And they all forsook **Him** and fled.

TIMELINE: JEREMIAH'S MINISTRY, ABOUT 627 TO 580 B.C.

*Jeremiah 23:5 Behold, the days come, saith the **LORD**, that **I** will raise unto David a **Righteous Branch**, and a **King** shall reign and prosper, and shall execute judgment and justice in the Earth.

*Jeremiah 30:9 But they shall serve the **LORD** their **God**, and David their King, whom **I** will raise up unto them.

*Jeremiah 31:15 Thus saith the **LORD**: "A voice was heard in Ramah, lamentation, and bitter weeping; Rachel weeping for her children, because they were not".

Genesis 42:13 And they said, "Thy servants are twelve brethren, the sons of one man in the land of Canaan; and behold, the youngest is this day with our father, and one is not".

Matthew 2:17, 18 Then was fulfilled that which was spoken by Jeremy the prophet, saying, 18)

'IN RAMAH, WAS THERE A VOICE HEARD, LAMENTATION AND WEEPING, AND GREAT MOURNING. RACHEL WEEPING FOR HER CHILDREN, AND WOULD NOT BE COMFORTED, BECAUSE THEY ARE NOT".

*Jeremiah 31:31 Behold, the days come, saith the **LORD**, that **I** will make a New Covenant with the House of Israel, and with the House of Judah:

God said....

Jeremiah 32:8 So Hanameel, mine uncle's son came to me in the court of the prison according to the Word of the **LORD**, and said unto me, "Buy my field, I pray thee, that is in Anathoth, which is in the country of Benjamin: for the right of inheritance is thine, and the redemption is thine; buy it for thyself". Then, I knew that this was the Word of the **LORD**.

Jeremiah 33:15 In those days, and at that time, will **I** cause the **Branch of Righteousness** to grow up into David; and **He** shall execute judgment and righteousness in the land.

Zechariah 6:12, 13 And speak unto him, saying, "Thus speaketh the **LORD** of Hosts, saying, "Behold the **Man Whose** Name is **The Branch**; and **He** shall grow up out of **His** place, and **He** shall build the Temple of the **LORD**: 13) Even **He** shall build the Temple of the **LORD**; and **He** shall bear the Glory, and shall sit and rule upon **His** Throne; and **He** shall be a Priest upon **His** Throne: and the Counsel of Peace shall be between them both".

Ezekiel 37:25 And they shall dwell in the land that **I** have given unto Jacob **My** servant, wherein your fathers have dwelt; and they shall dwell therein, even they, and their children, and their children's children for ever: and **My** servant David shall be their Prince forever.

Isaiah 60:21 Thy people also shall be all Righteous: they shall inherit the land for ever, the branch of **My** planting, the work of **My** hands, that **I** may be Glorified.

John 12:34 The people answered **Him**, we have heard out of the law that **Christ** abideth for ever: and how sayest **Thou**, The **Son** of Man must be lifted up? Who is this **Son** of Man?

Daniel 7:13, 14 I saw in the night visions, and behold, **One** like the **Son** of Man came with the clouds of Heaven, and came to the **Ancient** of **Days**, and they brought **Him** near before **Him**. 14) And there was given **Him** Dominion, and Glory, and a Kingdom, that all people, nations, and languages, should serve **Him**: **His** Dominion is an Everlasting Dominion, which shall not pass away, and **His** Kingdom that which shall not be destroyed.

☆Daniel 9:25 Know therefore and understand, that from the going forth of the commandment to restore and to build Jerusalem unto the **Messiah** the **Prince** shall be seven weeks, and threescore and two weeks: the street shall be built again, and the wall, even in troublous times.

John 1:41 He first findeth his own brother Simon, and saith unto him, "We have found the **Messias**, which is, being interpreted, The **Christ**".

Isaiah 55:4 Behold, **I** have given **Him** for a witness to the people, a Leader and a Commander to the people.

☆Daniel 9:26 After threescore and two weeks shall **Messiah** be cut off, but not for **Himself**: and the people of the prince that shall come shall destroy the city and the sanctuary; and the end thereof shall be with a flood, and unto the end of the war, desolations are determined. Matthew 27:50 **Jesus**, when **He** had cried again with a loud voice, yielded up the ghost.

☆Hosea 11:1 When Israel was a child, then **I** loved him, and called **My Son** out of Egypt.

☆Amos 9:11 In that day will **I** raise up the Tabernacle of David that is fallen, and close up the breaches thereof; and **I** will raise up his ruins, and **I** will build it as in the days of old:

☆Micah 5:2 But thou, Bethlehem Ephratah, though thou be little among thousands of Judah, yet out of thee shall **He** come forth unto **Me** that is to be **Ruler** in Israel; **Whose** goings forth have been from old, from everlasting.

Matthew 2:6 AND THOU BETHLEHEM, IN THE LAND OF JUDA, ART NOT THE LEAST AMONG THE PRINCES OF JUDA: FOR OUT OF THEE SHALL COME A **GOVERNOR**, THAT SHALL RULE **MY** PEOPLE ISRAEL.

Luke 2:4-7 And Joseph also went up from Galilee, out of the city of Nazareth, into Judaea, unto the city of David, which is called Bethlehem; (Because he was of the house and lineage of David); to be taxed with Mary his espoused wife, being great with **Child**. And so it was, that, while they were there, the days were accomplished that she should be delivered. And she brought forth her Firstborn **Son**, and wrapped **Him** in swaddling clothes, and laid **Him** in a manger; because there was no room for them in the inn.

Zechariah 3:8 Hear now, O Joshua the high priest, thou, and thy fellows that sit before thee: for they are men wondered at: for, Behold, **I** will bring forth **My Servant**, The **BRANCH**.

Isaiah 42:1 Behold **My Servant**, whom **I** uphold; **Mine Elect**, in whom **My Soul** delighteth, **I** have put **My Spirit** upon **Him**: **He** shall bring forth judgment to the Gentiles.

Zechariah 6:13 Even **He** shall build the Temple of the **LORD**; and **He** shall bear the Glory and shall sit and rule upon **His** Throne; and **He** shall be a Priest upon **His** Throne: and the Counsel of Peace shall be between them both.

Zechariah 9:9 Rejoice greatly, O daughter of Zion; shout, O daughter of Jerusalem: behold, thy **King** cometh unto thee: **He** is Just, and having Salvation; lowly, and riding upon an ass, and upon a colt, the foal of an ass.

Matthew 21:4, 5 All this was done, that it might be fulfilled which was spoken by the prophet, saying, 5) TELL YE THE DAUGHTER OF SION, BEHOLD, THY **KING** COMETH UNTO THEE, MEEK, AND SITTING UPON AN ASS, AND A COLT THE FOAL OF AN ASS.

Zechariah 9:10 And **I** will cut off the chariot from Ephraim, and the horse from Jerusalem, and the battle bow shall be cut off: and **He** shall speak peace unto the heathen: and **His** Dominion shall be from sea even to sea, and from the river even to the ends of the Earth.

Micah 4:2-4 And many nations shall come, and say, "Come, and let us go up to the Mountain of the **LORD**, and to the House of the **God** of Jacob; and **He** will teach us of **His** ways, and we will walk in **His** paths: for the law shall go forth of Zion, and the Word of the **LORD** from Jerusalem. 3) And **He** shall judge among many people, and rebuke strong nations afar off; and they shall beat their swords into plowshares, and their spears into pruning hooks: nation shall not lift up a sword against nation, neither shall they learn war any more. 4) But they shall sit every man under his vine and under his fig tree; and none shall make them afraid: for the mouth of the **LORD** of Hosts hath spoken it.

*Zechariah 11:13 And the **LORD** said unto me, "Cast it unto the potter": a goodly price that I was prised at of them. And I took the thirty pieces of silver and cast them to the potter in the house of the **LORD**.

Matthew 27:7 And they took counsel, and bought with them the potter's field, to bury strangers in.

Matthew 27:10 AND GAVE THEM FOR THE POTTER'S FIELD, AS THE **LORD** APPOINTED ME.

*Zechariah 13:7 Awake, O sword, against **My Shepherd**, and against the man that is **My Fellow**, saith the **LORD** of Hosts: smite the **Shepherd**, and the sheep shall be scattered: and **I** will turn **Mine** hand upon the little ones.

Matthew 26:56 "But all this was done, that the Scriptures of the prophets might be fulfilled", then all the disciples forsook **Him** and fled.

*Malachi 3:1 Behold, **I** will send **My** messenger, and **He** shall prepare the way before **Me**: and the **Lord**, whom ye seek, shall suddenly come to **His** Temple, even the **Messenger** of the Covenant, whom ye delight in; Behold, **He** shall come, saith the **Lord** of Hosts.

*Malachi 4:5 Behold, **I** will send you Elijah the prophet before the coming of the Great and Dreadful day of the **LORD**:

TIMELINE: 433 TO 400 B.C.

*Matthew 8:11 And **I** say unto you, "That many shall come from the east and the west, and shall sit down with Abraham, Isaac and Jacob, in the Kingdom of Heaven".

Isaiah 49:12 Behold, these shall come from far: and lo, these from the north and from the west; and these from the land of Sinim.

Isaiah 59:19 So shall they fear the Name of the **LORD** from the west, and **His** Glory from the rising of the sun. When the enemy shall come in like a flood, the **Spirit** of the **Lord** shall lift up a standard against him.

Ephesians 3:6 That the Gentiles should be fellow heirs, and of the same body, and partakers of **His** promise in **Christ** by the Gospel:

*Matthew 10:35 For **I** am come to set a man at variance against his father, and the daughter against her mother, and the daughter n law against her mother-in-law.

Micah 7:6 For the son dishonoureth the father, the daughter riseth up against her mother, the daughter in law against her mother-in-law; a man's enemies are the men of his own house.

*Matthew 16:27 For the **Son** of Man shall come in the Glory of **His Father** with **His** angels; and then **He** shall reward every man according to works.

*Matthew 20:28 Even as the **Son** of Man came not to be ministered unto, but to minister, and give. **His** life a ransom for many.

God said....

Isaiah 53:12 Therefore will **I** divide **Him** a portion with the great, and **He** shall divide the spoil with the strong; because **He** hath poured out **His Soul** unto death: and **He** was numbered with the transgressors; and **He** bare the sin of many and made intercession for the transgressors.

Matthew 21:42 **Jesus** saith unto them, "Did ye never read in the Scriptures? The **Stone** which the builders rejected, the same is become the **Head** of the Corner: this is the **LORD'S** doing, and it is marvelous in our eyes?

Matthew 21:44 And whosoever shall fall on this **Stone** shall be broken but on whomsoever it shall fall, it will grind him to powder.

Isaiah 8:14, 15 And **He** shall be for a Sanctuary, but for a Stone of Stumbling and for a Rock of Offence to both the Houses of Israel, for a gin and for a snare to the inhabitants of Jerusalem. A many among them shall stumble, and fall, and be broken, and be snared, and be taken.

Matthew 22:44 THE **LORD** SAID UNTO MY **LORD**, "SIT **THOU** ON **MY** RIGHT HAND, TILL **I** MAKE **THINE** ENEMIES **THY** FOOTSTOOL".

Matthew 23:39 For **I** say unto you, ye shall not see **Me** henceforth, till ye shall say BLESSED IS **HE** THAT COMETH IN THE NAME OF THE **LORD**.

Matthew 24:30 And then shall appear the sign of the **Son** of Man in Heaven: and then shall all the tribes of the Earth mourn, and they shall see the **Son** of Man coming in the clouds of Heaven with Power and great Glory.

Revelations 1:7 Behold, **He** cometh with clouds; and every eye shall see **Him**. And they also which pierced **Him**: and all kindreds of the Earth shall wail because of **Him**, even so…Amen.

Matthew 26:31 Then saith Jesus unto them, "All ye shall be offended because of **Me** this night: for it is written, **I** will smite the **Shepherd**, and the sheep of the flock shall be scattered abroad".

Matthew 26:56 "But all this was done, that the Scriptures of the prophets might be fulfilled. Then all the disciples forsook **Him** and fled".

Zechariah 13:7 Awake, O sword, against **My Shepherd**, and against the *Man* that is **My Fellow**, saith the **LORD** of Hosts: smite the **Shepherd**, and the sheep shall be scattered: and **I** will turn **Mine** hand upon the little ones.

⋆Mark 9:12 And **He** answered and told them, "Elias verily cometh first, and restoreth all things; and how it is written of the **Son** of Man, that **He** must suffer many things, and set at nought.

Psalm 22:6 But **I** am a worm, and no man; a reproach of men, and despised of the people.

Philippians 2:7 But made **Himself** of no reputation, and took upon **Him** in the form of a servant, and was made in the likeness of men:

⋆Mark 10:45 For even the **Son** of man came not to be ministered unto, but to minister, and to give **His** life a ransom for many.

Isaiah 53:12 Therefore will **I** divide **Him** a portion with the great, and **He** shall divide the spoil with the strong; because **He** hath poured out **His Soul** unto death: and **He** was numbered with the transgressors; and **He** bare the sin of many and made intercession for the transgressors.

⋆Mark 12:10 And have ye not read this Scripture; THE **STONE** WHICH THE BUILDERS REJECTED IS BECOME THE **HEAD** OF THE CORNER:

Psalm 118:22 The **Stone** which the builders refused is become the **Head Stone** of the Corner.

⋆Mark 12:36 For David himself said by the **Holy Ghost**, THE **LORD** SAID TO MY **LORD**, "SIT **THOU** ON **MY** RIGHT HAND, TILL **I** MAKE **THINE** ENEMIES **THY** FOOTSTOOL".

God said....

Psalm 110:1 The **LORD** said unto my **Lord**, "Sit **Thou** at **My** right hand, until **I** make **Thine** enemies **Thy** footstool".

Mark 14:27 And **Jesus** saith unto them, "All ye shall be offended because of **Me** this night: for it is written, '**I** WILL SMITE THE **SHEPHERD**, AND THE SHEEP SHALL BE SCATTERED'".

Zechariah 13:7 Awake, O sword, against **My Shepherd**, and against the *Man* that is **My Fellow**, saith the **LORD** of Hosts: smite the **Shepherd**, and the sheep shall be scattered: and I will turn **Mine** hand upon the little ones.

Luke 1:17 And he shall go before **Him** *in the* **Spirit** and *power* of Elias, to turn the hearts of the fathers to the children, and the disobedient to the wisdom of the just; to make ready a people prepared for the **Lord**.

Luke 1:33 And **He** shall reign over the House of Jacob forever; and of **His** Kingdom there shall be no end.

Luke 1:79 To give **Light** to them that sit in darkness and in the shadow of death, to guide our feet into the way of peace.

John 14:27 Peace **I** leave with you, **My** peace **I** give to you; not as the world gives do **I** give to you. Let not your heart be troubled, neither let it be afraid.

Luke 2:34 And Simeon blessed them, and said unto Mary **His** mother, "Behold, this **Child** is set for the fall and rising again of many in Israel; and for a sign which shall be spoken against.

Luke 13:35 Behold, your house is left to you desolate and verily **I** say unto you, "Ye shall not see **Me**, until the time come when ye shall say, 'Blessed is **He** that cometh in the Name of the **LORD**'".

Jeremiah 22:5 "But if ye will not hear these words, **I** swear by **Myself**", saith the **LORD**, "That this house shall become a desolation".

*Luke 20:17 And **He** beheld them, and said, "What is this then that is written, the **Stone** which the builders rejected, the same is become the **Head** of the Corner?

Isaiah 8:14, 15 And **He** shall be for a Sanctuary, but for a Stone of Stumbling and for a Rock of

Offence to both the Houses of Israel, for a gin and for a snare to the inhabitants of Jerusalem. And many among them shall stumble, and fall, and be broken, and be snared, and be taken.

*Luke 20:18 Whosoever shall fall upon the **Stone** shall be broken; but on whomsoever it shall fall, it will grind him to powder.

Luke 20:42 "And David himself saith in the Book of Psalm, 'The **LORD** said unto my **Lord**, sit **Thou** on **My** right hand'".

Psalm 110:1 The **LORD** said unto my **Lord**, "Sit **Thou** at **My** right hand, until **I** make **Thine** enemies **Thy** footstool.

*Luke 21:27 "And then shall they see the **Son** of Man coming in a cloud with Power and great Glory".

Revelation 1:7 "Behold, **He** cometh with clouds; and every eye shall see **Him**, and they also which pierced **Him**: and all kindreds of the Earth shall wall because of **Him**, even so…Amen".

Revelation 14:14 And I looked, and behold, a white cloud, and upon the cloud **One** sat like unto the **Son** of Man, having on **His** head, a golden crown, and in **His** hand a sharp sickle.

*Luke 22:37 "For **I** say unto you, that this is written, much yet be accomplished in **Me**, 'And **He** was reckoned among the transgressors: for the things concerning **Me** have an end".

Luke 23:32 And there were also two other malefactors, let with **Him** to be put to death.

God said....

Acts 3:20 And **He** shall send **Jesus Christ**, which before was preached unto you:

Malachi 3:1 "Behold! **I** will send **My Messenger**, and **He** shall prepare the way before **Me**: and the **Lord**, whom ye seek, shall suddenly come to **His** Temple, even the **Messenger** of the Covenant, whom ye delight in: Behold! **He** shall come", saith the **LORD** of Hosts.

Romans 11:26, 27 And so all Israel shall be saved: as it is written, "There shall come out of Sion, the **Deliverer**, and shall turn away ungodliness from Jacob": 27) "For this is **My** Covenant unto them, when **I** shall take away their sins".

Isaiah 59:20 And the **Redeemer** shall come to Zion, and unto them that turn from transgression in Jacob, saith the **LORD**.

Romans 14:11 For it is written, "AS **I** LIVE, SAITH THE **LORD**, EVERY KNEE SHALL BOW TO **ME**, AND EVERY TONGUE SHALL CONFESS TO **GOD**".

Romans 15:21 But as it is written, "To whom **He** was not spoken of, they shall see and they that have not heard shall understand".

1 Corinthians 15:26 The last enemy that shall be destroyed is death.

2 Timothy 1:10 But is now made manifest by the appearing of our **Saviour Jesus Christ**, who hath abolished death, and hath brought life and immortality to light through the gospel.

1 Corinthians 15:27 For **He** hath put all thins under **His** feet. But when **He** saith all things are put under **Him**, it is manifest that **He** is excepted, which did put all things under **Him**.

Psalm 8:6 **Thou** madest **Him** to have Dominion over the works of **Thy** hands; **Thou** hast put all things under **His** feet...

*2 Corinthians 5:10 For we must all appear before the judgment seat of **Christ**: that everyone may receive the things done in his body, according to that he hath done, whether it be good or bad.

*Philippians 2:11 And that every tongue should confess that **Jesus Christ is Lord**, to the Glory of **God the Father**.

Isaiah 45:23 **I** have sworn by **Myself**, in the Word is gone out of **My** mouth in *Righteousness*, and shall not return, that unto **Me** *every knee shall bow, every tongue shall swear.*

*Hebrew 10:37 FOR YET A LITTLE WHILE, AND **HE** THAT SHALL COME WILL COME! AND WILL NOT TARRY.

*Hebrew 12:28 Wherefore we are receiving a Kingdom which cannot be moved, let us have grace, whereby we may serve **God** acceptably with reverence and godly fear:

Daniel 2:44 And in the days of these kings shall the **God** of Heaven set up a Kingdom, which shall never be destroyed: and the Kingdom shall not be left to other people, but it shall break in pieces and consume all these kingdoms, and It shall stand for ever.

*2 Peter 3:10 But the day of the **LORD** will come as a thief in the night; in which the Heavens shall pass away, with a great noise, and the elements shall melt with fervent heat, the Earth also and the works that are therein shall be burned up.

*Matthew 24:43 But know this, that if the goodman of the house had known in what watch the thief would come, he would have watched, and would not have suffered his house to be broken up.

*Revelation 1:5 And from **Jesus Christ,** who is the faithful witness, and the **First Begotten** of the dead, and the **Prince** of the kings of the Earth, unto **Him** that loved us, and washed us from our sins in **His** own blood.

God said....

Psalm 89:27 Also **I** will make **Him My Firstborn**, Higher than the kings of the Earth.

Revelation 2:27 **He** shall rule them with a rod of iron; as the vessels of a potter shall they be broken to shivers: even as **I** received of **My Father**.

Psalm 2:8, 9 Ask of **Me**, and **I** shall give **Thee** the heathen for **Thine** inheritance, and the uttermost parts of the Earth for **Thy** possession. 9) **Thou** shalt break then with a rod of iron; **Thou** shalt dash them in pieces like a potter's vessel.

Revelation 7:16 They shall hunger no more, neither thirst anymore; neither shall the sun light on them, nor any heat.

Revelation 12:5 She brought forth a man **Child**, who was to rule all nations with a *rod of iron*: and her **Child** was caught up unto **God**, and to **His** Throne.

Revelation 16:15 "Behold! **I** come as a thief. Blessed is he that watcheth, and keepeth his garments, lest he walk naked, and they see his shame".

Revelation 19:13 **He** was clothed with a vesture dipped in blood: and **His** Name is called The **Word** *of* **God**.

Revelation 21:4 **God** shall wipe away all tears from their eyes; and there shall be no more death, neither sorrow, nor crying neither shall there be any more pain: for the former things are passed away.

Isaiah 25:8 **He** will swallow up death in victory; and the **LORD God** will wipe away tears from off all faces; and the rebuke of **His** people shall **He** take away from off all the Earth: for the **LORD** hath spoken it.

Isaiah 35:10 The ransomed of the **LORD** shall return and come to Zion with songs and everlasting joy upon their heads: They shall obtain joy and gladness, and sorrow and sighing shall flee away.

*Revelation 22:12 "And Behold! **I** come quickly; and **My** reward is with **Me**, to give every man according as his work shall be.

Isaiah 40:10 "Behold! The **LORD God** will come with a strong hand, and **His** arm shall rule for **Him**: Behold! **His** reward is with **Him**, and **His** work before **Him**.

Revelation 20:12 I saw the dead, small and great, stand **God**; and the books were opened: and another book was opened, which is the Book of Life: and the dead were judged out of those things which were written in the books, according to their works.

TIMELINE: ABOUT 520 TO 518 B.C.

*Zechariah 12:10 And **I** will pour upon the House of David, and upon the inhabitants of Jerusalem, the **Spirit** of Grace and of Supplications: and they shall look upon **Me** whom they have pierced, and they shall mourn for **Him**, as one mourneth for his only son, and shall be in bitterness for his firstborn.

TIMELINE WITHIN 433 TO 400 B.C.

*Matthew 1:1 The book of the generation of **Jesus Christ**, the **Son** of David, the **Son** of Abraham.

Acts 2:30, Therefore being a prophet, and knowing that **God** had sworn with an oath to him, that the fruit of his loins, according to the flesh, **He** would raise up **Christ** to sit on his Throne;

*Matthew 1:6 And Jesse begat David the king; and David the king begat Solomon of her that had been the wife of Urais…

1 Samuel 16:1 And the **LORD** said unto Samuel, "How long wilt thou mourn for Saul, seeing **I** have rejected him from reigning over Israel? Fill thine horn with oil, and go, **I** will send thee to Jesse the Bethlehemite: for **I** have provided **Me** a king among his sons".

*Matthew 1:18 Now the birth of **Jesus Christ** was on this wise: When as **His** mother Mary was espoused to Joseph, before they came together, she was found with child of the **Holy Ghost**.

*Matthew 1:23 BEHOLD, A VIRGIN SHALL BE WITH CHILD, AND SHALL BRING FORTH A **SON**, AND THEY SHALL CALL **HIS** NAME **EMMANUEL**, WHICH BEING INTERPRETED IS, **GOD** WITH US.

*Matthew 2:1 Now when **Jesus** was born in Bethlehem of Judaea in the days of Herod the king, behold, there came wise men from the east to Jerusalem…

God said....

Micah 5:2 But thou, Bethlehem Ephratah, though thou be little among the thousands of Judah, yet out of thee shall **He** come forth unto **Me** that is to be **Ruler** in Israel; *whose* goings forth have been from Old, from Everlasting.

1 King 4:30 And Solomon's wisdom excelled the wisdom of all the children of the east country, and all the wisdom of Egypt.

*Matthew 2:6 AND THOU BETHLEHEM, IN THE LAND OF JUDA, ART NOT THE LEAST AMONG THE PRINCES OF JUDA: FOR OUT OF THEE SHALL COME A **GOVERNOR**, THAT SHALL RULE **MY** PEOPLE ISRAEL.

Genesis 49:10 The Sceptre shall not depart from Judah, nor a lawgiver from between his feet, until **Shiloh** come; and unto **Him** shall the gathering of the people be.

*Matthew 2:14, 15 When he arose, he took the young *child* and **His** mother by night and departed into Egypt: 15) And was there until the death of Herod: that it might be fulfilled which was spoken of the **LORD** by the prophet, saying, "OUT OF EGYPT, HAVE **I** CALLED **MY SON**".

*Matthew 2:18 IN RAMA WAS THERE A VOICE HEARD, LAMENTATION, AND WEEPING, AND GREAT MOURNING, RACHEL WEEPING FOR HER CHILDREN, AND WOULD NOT BE COMFORTED, BECAUSE THEY ARE NOT.

Jeremiah 31:15 Thus saith the **LORD**; a voice was heard in Ramah, lamentation, and bitter weeping; Rachel weeping for her children refused to be comforted for her children, because they were not.

*Matthew 2:23 And **He** came and dwelt in a city called Nazareth: that it might be fulfilled which was spoken by the prophets, **He** shall be called a Nazarene.

John 1:45 Philip findeth Nathanael, and saith unto him, "We have found **Him**, of whom Moses in the law, and the prophets, did write, **Jesus** of Nazareth, the **Son** of Joseph".

Judge 13:5 For, lo, thou shalt conceive, and bear a **Son**; and no razor shall come on **His** head: for the **Child** shall be a Nazarite unto **God** from the womb: and **He** shall begin to deliver Israel out of the hand of the Philistines.

*Matthew 3:3 For this is **He** that was spoken of by the prophet Esaias, saying, "THE VOICE OF ONE CRYING IN THE WILDERNESS, PREPARE YE THE WAY OF THE **LORD**, MAKE **HIS** PATHS STRAIGHT".

*Matthew 3:11 "I indeed baptize you with water unto repentance: but **He** that cometh after me is mightier than I, **whose** shoes I am not worthy to bear: **He** shall baptize you with the **Holy Ghost**, and with Fire":

Acts 2:4 And they were all filled with the **Holy Ghost**, and began to speak with other tongues, as the **Spirit** gave them utterance.

Acts 2:33 Therefore being by the right hand of **God**, exalted and having received of the **Father**, the promise of the **Holy Ghost**, **He** hath shed forth this, which ye now see and hear.

*Matthew 3:16, 17 And **Jesus**, when **He** was baptized, went up straightway out of the water: and lo, the Heavens were opened unto **Him**, and **He** saw the **Spirit** of **God** descending like a dove, and lighting upon **Him**:

Isaiah 11:2 And the **Spirit** of the **LORD**, shall rest upon **Him**, the **Spirit** of Wisdom, and

Understanding, the **Spirit** of Counsel and Might, the **Spirit** of Knowledge and of the fear of the **LORD**;

God said....

Isaiah 42:1 Behold, **My Servant**, whom **I** uphold; **Mine Elect**, in **whom My Soul** delighteth; **I** have put **My Spirit** upon **Him**: **He** shall bring forth judgement to the Gentiles.

*Matthew 4:13 And leaving Nazareth, **He** came and dwelt in Capernaum, which is upon the sea coast, in the borders of Zabulon and Nephthalim:

*Matthew 8:17 That it might be fulfilled which was spoken by Esaias the prophet, saying, **Himself** took our infirmities, and bare our sicknesses.

*Matthew 11:5 The blind receives their sight, and the lame walk, the lepers are cleansed, and the deaf hear; the dead are raised up, and the poor have the gospel preached to them.

*Matthew 11:10 For this is he, of whom it is written, "Behold, **I** send **My** messenger before **Thy** face, which shall prepare **Thy** way before **Thee**".

*Matthew 11:13 "For all the prophets and the law prophesied until John"

*Matthew 12:18 "Behold **My Servant**, whom **I** have chosen; **Me Beloved**, in whom **My Soul** is well pleased: **I** will put **My Spirit** upon **Him**, and **He** shall shew judgment to the Gentiles.

*Matthew 13:14 "And in them is fulfilled the prophecy of Esaias, which saith, "By hearing ye shall hear, and shall not understand; and seeing ye shall see, and shall not perceive:

*Matthew 13:34 All these things spake **Jesus** unto the multitude in parables; and without a parable spake **He** not unto them:

*Matthew 15:8 "This people draweth nigh unto **Me** with their mouth, and honoureth **Me** with their lips; but their heart is far from **Me**.

*Matthew 17:5 While **He** yet spake, behold, *a bright cloud* overshadowed them: and behold a **Voice** out of the cloud, which said, "This is **My Beloved Son**, in whom **I** am well pleased; hear ye **Him**".

Isaiah 42:1 Behold! **My Servant**, whom **I** uphold; **Mine Elect**, in whom **My Soul** delighteth; **I** have put **My Spirit** upon **Him**: **He** shall bring forth judgment to the Gentiles.

2 Peter 1:17 For **He** received from **God** the **Father**, honour and glory, when there came such a **Voice** to **Him** from the Excellent Glory, "This is **My Beloved Son**, in whom, **I** am well pleased.

*Matthew 21:5 Tell ye the daughter of Sion, "Behold, thy **King** cometh unto thee, meek, and sitting upon an ass, and a colt the foal of an ass.

*Matthew 21:9 And the multitudes that went before, and that followed, cried, saying, "Hosanna to the **Son** of David: Blessed is **He** that cometh in the Name of the **LORD**; Hosanna in the hightest".

Psalm 118:26 Blessed be **He** that cometh in the Name of the **LORD**: we have blessed you out of the House of the **LORD**.

Matthew 23:39 For **I** say unto you, ye shall not see **Me** henceforth, till ye shall say, "Blessed is **He** that cometh in the Name of the **LORD**".

*Matthew 21:12 And **Jesus** went into the Temple of **God**, and cast out all them that sold and bought in the Temple, and overthrew the tables of the moneychangers, and the seats of them that sold doves,

Malachi 3:1 Behold, **I** will send **My** messenger, and he shall prepare the way before **Me**: and the **Lord**, whom you seek, shall suddenly come to **His** Temple, even the **Messenger** of the Covenant, whom ye delight in: Behold! "**He** shall come, saith the **LORD** of Hosts".

*Matthew 21:15 And when the chief priests and scribes saw the wonderful things that **He** did, and the children crying in the Temple, and saying, "Hosanna, to the **Son** of David"; they were sore displeased...

*Matthew 26:14 Then one of the twelve, called Judas Iscariot, went unto the chief priests,

God said....

Matthew 10:4 Simon the Canaanite, and Judas Iscariot, who also betrayed **Him**.

*Matthew 26:42 **He** went away again the second time, and praying, saying, "O **My Father**, if this cup may not pass away from **Me**, except **I** drink it, **Thy** will be done".

Isaiah 50:5-7 The **LORD GOD** hath opened **Mine** ear, and **I** was not rebellious, neither turned away back. **I** gave **My** back to the smiters, and **My** cheeks to them that plucked off the hair: **I** hid not **My** face from shame and spitting. For the **LORD GOD** will help **Me**; therefore, shall **I** not be confounded: therefore, have **I** set **My** face like a flint, and **I** know that **I** shall not be ashamed.

*Matthew 26:60 But found none: yea, though many false witnesses came, yet found them none. At the last came two false witnesses,

Psalm 27:12 Deliver **Me** not over unto the will of **Mine** enemies: for false witnesses are risen up against **Me**, and such as breathe out cruelty.

*Matthew 26:67 Then did they spit on **His** face and buffeted **Him**; and others smote **Him** with the palms of their hands.

*Matthew 27:9 Then was fulfilled that which was spoken by Jeremiah the prophet, saying, "And they took the thirty pieces of silver, the price of **Him** that was valued, whom they of the children of Israel did value,

*Matthew 27:14 And **He** answered him to never a word; insomuch that the Governor marveled greatly.

Psalm 38:13, 14 But **I** as a deaf man, heard not; and **I** was as a dumb man that openeth not his mouth. 14) Thus, **I** was a man that heareth not, and in whose mouth are no reproofs.

*Matthew 27:26 Then released he, Barabbas unto them: and when he had scourged **Jesus**, he delivered **Him** to be crucified.

Isaiah 50:6 **I** gave **My** back to the smiters, and **My** cheeks to them that plucked off the hair: **I** hid not **My** face from shame and spitting.

*Matthew 27:30 And they spit upon **Him**, and took the reed, and smote **Him** on the head.

*Matthew 27:34 They gave **Him** vinegar to drink, mingled with gall: and when **He** had tasted thereof, **He** would not drink.

Psalm 69:21 They gave **Me** also gall for **My** meat; and in **My** thirst they gave **Me** vinegar to drink.

*Matthew 27:35 And they crucified **Him**, and parted **His** garments, casting lots: that it might be fulfilled which was spoken by the prophet, THEY PARTED **MY** GARMENTS AMONG THEM, AND UPON **MY** VESTURE DID THEY CAST LOTS.

*Matthew 27:36 And sitting down they watched **Him** there.

Matthew 27:54 Now when the centurion, and they that were with him watching **Jesus**, saw the earthquake, and those things that were done, they feared greatly, saying, "Truly this was the **Son** of **God**".

Psalm 22:17 **I** may tell all **My** bones: they look and stare upon **Me**.

*Matthew 27:39 And they that passed by reviled **Him**, wagging their heads...

*Matthew 27:42 "**He** saved others; **Himself, He** cannot save". "If **He** be the **King** of Israel, let **Him** now come down from the cross, and we will believe **Him**".

*Matthew 27:46 And about the ninth hour, **Jesus** cried with a loud voice, saying, "**ELI, ELI, LAMA SABACHTHANI**"? That is to say, "**MY GOD, MY GOD**, WHY HAST **THOU** FORSAKEN **ME**"?

God said....

Psalm 22:1 "**MY GOD**, **MY GOD**, WHY HAST **THOU** FORSAKEN **ME**? Why art **THOU** so far from helping **Me**, and from the words of **My** roaring?

*Matthew 27:57 When the even was come, there came a rich man of Arimathea, named Joseph, who also himself was **Jesus**' disciple:

TIMELINE: ABOUT 60 A.D.

*Mark 1:2 As it is written in the Prophets, "Behold, **I** send **My** messenger before **Thy** face, which shall prepare **Thy** way before thee.

Malachi 3:1 "Behold, **I** will send **My** messenger, and he shall prepare the way before **Me**: and the **Lord**, whom ye seek, shall suddenly come to **His** Temple, even the **Messenger** of the Covenant, whom ye delight in: behold, **He** shall come", saith the **Lord** of Hosts.

*Mark 1:3, 4 The voice of one crying in the wilderness, "Prepare ye the way of the **Lord**, and make **His** paths straight". John did baptize in the wilderness and preach the baptism of repentance for the remission of sins.

*Mark 3:6 And the Pharisees went forth, and straightaway took counsel with the Herodians against **Him**, how they might destroy **Him**.

Matthew 22:16 And they sent out unto **Him**, their disciples with the Herodians, saying, "**Master**, we know that **Thou** art true, and teachest the way of **God** in truth, neither carest **Thou** for any man: for **Thou** regardest not the person of men.

*Matthew 4:12 That seeing they may see, and not perceive; and hearing they may hear, and not understand; lest at any time they should be converted, and their sins should be forgiven them.

Isaiah 6:9 And **He** said, "Go, and tell this people, hear ye indeed, but understand not; and see ye indeed, but perceive not.

Mark 7:6 **He** answered and said unto them, "Well hath Esaias prophesied of you hypocrites, as it is written, 'this people honoureth **Me** with their lips, but their heart is far from **Me**. Howbeit in vain do they worship **Me**, teaching for doctrines the commandments of men'".

Isaiah 29:13 Wherefore the **Lord** said, "Forasmuch as this people draw near **Me** with their mouth, and with their lips do honour **Me**, but have removed their heart far from **Me**, and their fear toward **Me** is taught by the precept of men:

*Mark 9:7 And there was a cloud that overshadowed them: and a **Voice** came out of the cloud, saying, "This is **My Beloved Son**: hear **Him**".

Psalm 2:7 **I** will declare the decree: the **Lord** hath said unto **Me**, **Thou** *art* **My Son**; this day have **I Begotten Thee**.

*Mark 11:7 And they brought the colt to **Jesus** and cast their garments on him; and **He** sat upon him.

Zechariah 9:9 Rejoice greatly, O daughter of Zion; shout, O daughter of Jerusalem: behold, thy **King** cometh unto thee: **He** is Just, and having Salvation; lowly, and riding upon an ass, and upon a colt the foal of an ass.

*Mark 14:36 And **He** said, "**Abba**, **Father**, all things are possible unto **Thee**; take away this cup from **Me**: nevertheless, not what **I** will, but what **Thou** wilt".

*Mark 14:57, 58 And there arose certain, and bare false witness against **Him**, saying, 58) "We heard **Him** say, 'I will destroy this temple that is made with hands, and within three days, **I** will build **Another** made without hands'".

Psalm 27:12 Deliver **me** not over unto the will of **mine** enemies: for false witnesses are risen up against **me**, and such as breathe out cruelty.

Psalm 35:11 False witnesses did rise up; they laid to **my** charge, things that **I** knew not.

*Mark 14:65 And some began to spit on **Him**, and to cover **His** face, and to buffet **Him**, and to say unto **Him**, "Prophesy: and the servants did strike **Him** with the palms of their hands.

*Mark 15:1 And straightway in the morning the chief priests held a consultation with the elders and scribes and the whole council, and bound **Jesus**, and carried **Him** away, and delivered **Him** to Pilate.

Isaiah 53:7 **He** was oppressed, and **He** was afflicted, yet, **He** opened not **His** mouth: **He** is brought as a lamb to the slaughter, and as a sheep before her shearers is dumb, so **He** openeth not **His** mouth.

*Mark 15:3 And the chief priests accused **Him** of many things: but **He** answered nothing.

*Mark 15:19 And they smote **Him** on the head with a reed, and did spit upon Him, and bowing their knees worshipped **Him**.

Isaiah 52:14 As many were astonished at **Thee**; **His** visage was so marred more than any man, and **His** form more than the sons of men:

Micah 5:1 Now gather thyself in troops, O daughter of troops: He hath laid siege against us: they shall smite the **Judge** of Israel with a rod upon the cheek.

*Mark 15:27 And with **Him** they crucify two thieves: the one on **His** right hand, and the other on **His** left.

Isaiah 53:9 And **He** made **His** grave with the wicked, and with the rich, in **His** death; because **He** had done no violence, neither was any deceit in **His** mouth.

Isaiah 53:12 Therefore, will **I** divide **Him** a portion with the *Great*, and **He** shall divide the spoil with the *Strong*, because **He** hath poured out **His** **Soul** unto death: and **He** was numbered with the transgressors, and **He** bare the sin of many and made intercession for the transgressors.

God said....

*Mark 15:28 And so Pilate, willing to content the people, released Barabbas unto them, and delivered **Jesus**, when he had scourged **Him** to be crucified.

Isaiah 53:12 Therefore will **I** divide **Him** a portion with the great, and **He** shall divide the spoil with the strong; because **He** hath poured out **His Soul** unto death: and **He** was numbered with the transgressors; and **He** bare the sin of many and made intercession for the transgressors.

*Mark 15:29 And they that passed by railed on **Him**, wagging their heads, and saying, "Ah, **Thou** that destroyest the temple, and buildest it in three days,

*Mark 15:30 Save **Thyself** and come down from the cross".

Psalm 22:8 **He** trusted on the **LORD** that **He** would deliver **Him**: let **Him** deliver **Him**, seeing **He** delighteth in **Him**.

*Mark 15:31 Likewise also the chief priests mocking said among themselves with the scribes, "**He** saved others; **Himself, He** cannot save".

Psalm 69:19 **Thou** hast known **my** reproach, and **my** shame, and **my** dishonour: **mine** adversaries are all before **Thee**.

*Mark 15:33 And when the sixth hour was come, there was darkness over the whole land until the ninth hour.

*Mark 15:34 And at the ninth hour **Jesus** cried with a loud voice, saying, "**Eloi, Eloi, lama sabachthani**"? Which is being interpreted, "**My God, My God**, why hast **Thou** forsaken **Me**?".

Psalm 22:1 "**My GOD, My GOD**, why hast **Thou** forsaken **Me**? Why art **Thou** so far from helping **Me**?"

*Mark 15:36 And one ran and filled a spunge full of vinegar, and put it on a reed, and gave **Him** to drink, saying, "Let alone; let us see whether Elias will come to take **Him** down".

Psalm 69:21 "They gave **Me** also gall for **My** meat; and in **My** thirst they gave **Me** vinegar to drink".

*Mark 15:45 And when he knew it of the centurion, he gave the **body** to Joseph.

*Mark 16:6 And he saith unto them, "Be not affrighted: Ye seek **Jesus** of Nazareth, which was crucified: **He** is risen; **He** is not here: behold the place where they laid **Him**.

Hosea 6:2 After two days will **He** revive us: in the third day **He** will raise us up, and we shall live in **His** sight.

*Mark 16:19 So then after the **Lord** had spoken unto them, **He** was received up into Heaven, and sat on the right hand of **God**.

Isaiah 9:7 Of the increase of **His** Government and Peace there shall be no end, upon the Throne of David, and upon **His** Kingdom, to order it, and to establish it with the judgment and with justice from henceforth even forever. The zeal of the **Lord** of Hosts will perform this.

*Luke 1:26 And in the sixth month the angel Gabriel was sent from **God** unto a city of Galilee, named Nazareth.

*Luke 1:31 And, behold, thou shalt conceive in thy womb, and bring forth a **Son**, and shalt call **His** Name **JESUS**.

*Luke 2:1 And it came to pass in those days, that there went out a decree from Caesar Augustus, that all the world should be taxed.

*Luke 2:4 And Joseph also went up from Galilee, out of the city of Nazareth, in Judaea, unto the city of David, which is called Bethlehem; (because he was of the House and Lineage of David)

Micah 5:2 But thou, Bethlehem Ephratah, though thou be little among the thousands of Judah, yet out of thee shall **He** come forth unto **Me** that

God said....

is to be **Ruler** in Israel; **whose** goings forth have been from of old, from everlasting.

*Luke 2:11 For unto you is born this day in the city of David, **a Saviour**, which is **Christ** the **Lord**.

Philippians 2:11 And that every tongue should confess that **Jesus Christ** is **Lord**, to the glory of **God** the **Father**.

*Luke 2:32 A **Light** to lighten the Gentiles, and the Glory of **Thy** people Israel.

*Luke 3:3 And he came into all the country about Jordan, preaching the baptism of repentance for the remission of sins.

Luke 1:17 And he shall go before **Him** in the spirit and power of Elias, to turn the hearts of the fathers to the children, and the disobedient to the wisdom of the just; to make ready a people prepared for the **LORD**.

Luke 1:77 To give knowledge of Salvation unto **His** people by the remission of their sins.

*Luke 3:31 Which was the son of Melea, which was the son of Menan, which was the son of Mattatha, which was the son of Nathan, which was the **Son** of David,

Isaiah 9:7 Of the Increase of **His** Government and Peace there shall be no end, upon the Throne of David, and upon **His** Kingdom, to order it, and to establish it with judgment and with justice from henceforth even forever. The zeal of the **Lord** of Hosts will perform this.

*Luke 3:33 Which was the son of Aminadab, which was the son of Aram, which was the son of Esrom, which was the son of Phares, which was the son of Judah,

Genesis 49:10 The Sceptre shall not depart from Judah, nor a lawgiver from between his feet, until **Shiloh** come; and unto **Him** shall the gatherings of the people be.

*Luke 4:18, 19 THE **SPIRIT** *OF THE* **LORD** *IS UPON* **ME**, BECAUSE **HE** HATH ANOINTED **ME** TO

PREACH THE GOSPEL TO THE POOR; **HE** HATH SENT **ME** TO HEAL THE BROKENHEARTED, TO PREACH DELIVERANCE TO THE CAPTIVES, AND RECOVERING OF SIGHT TO THE BLIND, TO SET AT LIBERTY THEM THAT ARE BRUISED, TO PREACH THE ACCEPTABLE YEAR OF THE **LORD**.

*Luke 7:22 Then **Jesus** answering said unto them, "Go your way, and tell John what things ye have seen and heard; how that the blind see, the lame walk, the lepers are cleansed, the deaf hear, the dead are raised, to the poor the gospel is preached".

Isaiah 35:5 Then the eyes of the blind shall be opened, and the ears of the deaf shall be unstopped.

Isaiah 61:1 The **Spirit** of the **LORD GOD** is upon **Me**; because the **LORD** hath anointed **Me** to preach good tidings unto the meek; **He** hath sent **Me** to bind up the brokenhearted, to proclaim liberty to the captives, and the opening of the prison to them that are bound.

*Luke 8:10 And **He** said, "Unto you it is given to know the mysteries of the Kingdom of **God**: but to others in parables; that seeing they might not see and hearing they might not understand".

Isaiah 6:9 And **He** said, "Go, and tell this people, hear ye indeed, but understand not; and see ye indeed, but perceive not".

*Luke 19:38 Saying, "Blessed be the **King** that cometh in the Name of the **Lord**: peace in Heaven, and glory to the Highest".

God said....

Psalm 118:26 "Blessed be he that cometh in the Name of the **LORD**: we have blessed you out of the House of the **LORD**".

*Luke 22:42 Saying, "**Father**, if **Thou** be willing, remove this cup from **Me**: nevertheless, not **My** will, but **Thine**, be done".

Isaiah 50:5 The **LORD GOD** hath opened **Mine** ear, and **I** was not rebellious, neither turned away back.

*Luke 22:47, 48 And while **He** yet spake, behold a multitude, and he that was called Judas, one of the twelve, went before them, and drew near unto **Jesus** to kiss **Him**. 48) But **Jesus** said unto him, "Judas, betrayeth **Thou**, the **Son** of Man, with a kiss?"

*Luke 22:65 And many other things blasphemously spake they against **Him.**

Isaiah 53:3 **He** is despised and rejected of men; a **Man** sorrows, and aquainted with grief: and we hid as it were our faces from **Him**; **He** was despised, and we esteemed **Him** not.

*Luke 23:9 Then he questioned with **Him** in many words; but **He** answered him nothing.

*Luke 23:18 And they cried out all at once, saying, "Away with this **Man**, and release unto us Barabbas":

Acts 3:14 But ye denied the **Holy One** and the **Just** and desired a murderer to be granted unto you.

*Luke 23:32 And there were also two other malefactors, led with **Him** to be put to death.

*Luke 23:35 And the people stood beholding. And the rulers also with them, derided **Him**, saying, "**He** saved others; let **Him** save **Himself**, if **He** be **Christ**, the chosen of **God**".

Psalm 22:7, 8 All they that see **Me**, laugh **Me** to scorn: they shoot out the lip, they shake the head, saying, 8) "**He** trusted on the **LORD** that **He** would deliver **Him**: let **Him** deliver **Him**, seeing **He** delighted in **Him**".

*Luke 23:36 And the soldiers also mocked **Him**, coming to **Him**, and offering **Him** vinegar...

*Luke 23:44 And it was about the sixth hour, and there was a darkness over all the Earth until the ninth hour.

*Luke 23:53 And he took **It** down, and wrapped **It** in linen, and laid **It** in a sepulcher that was hewn in stone, wherein never man before was laid.

*Luke 24:51 And it came to pass, while **He** blessed them, **He** was parted from them, and carried up into Heaven.

TIMELINE: TOWARDS THE END OF THE 1ST CENTURY, A.D.

*John 1:11 **He** came unto **His** own, and **His** own received **Him** not.

Luke 19:14 But his citizens hated **Him**, and sent a message after **Him**, saying, "We will not have this **Man** to reign over us".

*John 1:23 He said, "I am the voice of one crying in the wilderness, make straight the way of the **LORD**, as said the prophet Esaias".

Isaiah 40:3 The voice of him that crieth in the wilderness, "Prepare ye the way of the **LORD**, make straight in the desert a highway for our **God**".

*John 1:33, 34 "And I knew **Him** not: but **He** that sent me to baptize with water, the same said unto me, 'Upon whom thou shalt see the **Spirit** descending, and remaining on **Him**, the same is **He** which baptizeth with the **Holy Ghost**. 34) And I saw, and bare record that this is the **Son** of **God**'".

*John 2:14 And found in the Temple those that sold oxen and sheep and doves, and the changers of money sitting:

*John 2:17 And **His** disciples remembered that it was written, "The zeal of **Thine** house hath eaten **Me** up".

*John 3:34 For **He** whom **God** hath sent, speaketh the words of **God**: for **God** giveth not the **Spirit** by measure unto **Him**.

God said....

Deuteronomy 18:18 **I** will raise up a **Prophet** from among their brethren, like unto thee, and will put **My** words in **His** mouth; and **He** shall speak unto them all that **I** shall command **Him**.

*John 7:5 For neither did **His** brethren believe in **Him**.

Micah 7:6 For the son dishonoureth the father, the daughter riseth up against her mother-inlaw; a man's enemies are the men of his own house.

Mark 3:21 And when **His** friends heard of it, they went out to lay hold on **Him**: for they said, "**He** is beside **Himself**".

*John 7:14 Now about the midst of the feast, **Jesus** went up into the Temple and taught.

Psalm 22:22 **I** will declare **Thy** Name unto **My** brethren: in the midst of the congregation will **I** praise **Thee**.

*John 12:13 Took branches of palm trees, and went forth to meet **Him**, and cried, "Hosanna: Blessed is the **King** of Israel that cometh in the Name of the **LORD**".

Psalm 118:26 Blessed be **He** that cometh in the Name of the **LORD**: we have blessed you out of the House of the **LORD**.

*John 12:15 Fear not, daughter of Sion: Behold! thy **King** cometh, sitting on an ass's colt.

*John 12:37 But though **He** had done so many miracles before them, yet they believed not on **Him**:

*John 12:40 **He** HATH BLINDED THEIR EYES AND HARDENED THEIR HEART; THAT THEY SHOULD NOT SEE WITH THEIR EYES, NOR UNDERSTAND WITH THEIR HEART, AND BE CONVERTED, AND **I** SHOULD HEAL THEM.

*John 13:18 **I** speak not of you all: **I** know whom **I** have chosen but that the Scripture may be fulfilled, he that eateth bread with **Me** hath lifted up his heel against **Me**.

Psalm 41:9 Yea, **Mine** own familiar friend, in whom **I** trusted, which did eat of **My** bread, hath lifted up his heel against **Me**.

*John 14:31 But that the world may know that **I** love the **Father**; and as the **Father** gave **Me** commandment, even so **I** do. Araise! Let us go hence.

John 10:18 No man taketh it from **Me**, but **I** lay it down of **Myself**. **I** have power to lay it down, and **I** have power to take it again. This commandment have **I** received of **My Father**.

*John 15:24 If **I** had not done among them the works which none other man did, they had not had sin: but now have they both seen and hated both **Me** and **My Father**.

*John 17:8 For **I** have given unto them the words which **Thou** gavest **Me**; and they have received them, and have known surely that **I** came out from **Thee**, and they have believed that **Thou** didst sent **Me**.

Deuteronomy 18:18 **I** will raise them up a **Prophet** from among their brethren, like unto thee, and will put **My** words in **His** mouth; and **He** shall speak unto them all that **I** shall command **Him**.

*John 18:40 Then cried they all again, saying, "Not this **Man**, but Barabbas". Now Barabbas was a robber.

*John 19:9 And went again into the judgment hall, and saith unto **Jesus**, "Whence art **Thou**?", but **Jesus** gave him no answer.

Psalm 38;13, 14 But **I**, as a deaf man, heard not; and **I** was a dumb man that openeth not his mouth. 14) Thus, **I** was as a man that heareth not, and in whose mouth are no reproofs.

God said....

Isaiah 53:7 **He** was oppressed, and **He** was afflicted, yet **He** opened not **His** mouth: **He** is brought as a lamb to the slaughter, and as a sheep before her shearers is dumb, so **He** openeth not **His** mouth.

*John 19:18 Where they crucified **Him**, and two others with **Him**, on either side one, and **Jesus** in the midst.

Matthew 20:19 And shall deliver **Him** to the Gentiles to mock, and to scourge, and to crucify **Him**: and the third day **He** shall rise again.

*John 19:24 They said therefore among themselves, "Let us not rend it, but cast lots for it, whose it shall be": that the Scriptures might be fulfilled, which saith, "They parted **My** rainment among them, and for **My** vesture they did cast lots". These things therefore the soldiers did.

Psalm 22:18 "They part **My** garments among them and cast lots upon **My** vesture".

*John 19:29 Now there was set a vessel full of vinegar: and they filled a sponge with vinegar, and put it upon hyssop, and put it to **His** mouth.

Psalm 69:21 They gave **Me** also gall for **My** meat; and in **My** thirst, they gave **Me** vinegar to drink.

*John 19:32 Then came the soldiers, and brake the legs of the first, and of the other which was crucified with **Him**.

*John 19:36 For these things were done, that the Scripture should be fulfilled, an "A bone of **Him** shall not be broken".

*John 19:37 And again another Scripture saith, "They shall look on **Him** whom they pierced".

Zechariah 12:10 And **I** will pour upon the House of David, and upon the inhabitants of Jerusalem, the **Spirit** of Grace and of supplications: and they shall look upon **Me** whom they have pierced, and they shall mourn for **Him**, as one mourneth for his only son, and shall be in bitterness for **Him**, as one that is in bitterness for *his* firstborn.

*John 20:27 Then saith **He** to Thomas, "Reach hither thy finger, and behold **My** hands; and reach hither thy hand and thrust it into **My** side: and be not faithless but believing".

TIMELINE: 63 A.D. TO 67 A.D.

*Acts 1:16 Men and brethren, this Scripture must needs have been fulfilled, which the **Holy Ghost** by the mouth of David spake before concerning Judas, which was guide to them that took **Jesus**.

Psalm 41:9 Yea, **Mine** own familiar friend, in whom **I** trusted, which did eat of **My** bread, hath lifted up his heel against **Me**.

Luke 22:47 And while **He** yet spake, behold a multitude, and he that was called Judas, one of the twelve, went before them, and drew near unto **Jesus** to kiss **Him**.

*Acts 1:20 For it is written in the Book of Psalm, "Let his habitation be desolate, and let no man dwell therein: and his bishoprick let another take".

Psalm 69:25 Let their habitation be desolate; and let none dwell in their tents.

Psalm 109:8 Let his days be few and let another take his office.

*Acts 2:22 Ye men of Israel, hear these words; **Jesus** of Nazareth, a Man approved of **God** among you by miracles and wonders and signs, which **God** did by **Him** in the midst of you, as ye yourselves also know:

Isaiah 50:5 The **LORD God** hath opened **Mine** ear, and **I** was not rebellious neither turned away back.

God said....

*Acts 2:25 For David speaketh concerning **Him**, I FORESAW THE **LORD** ALWAYS BEFORE MY FACE, FOR **HE** IS ON **MY** RIGHT HAND, THAT I SHOULD NOT BE MOVED:

*Acts 2:31 He seeing this before, spake of the resurrection of **Christ**, that **His Soul** was not left in hell, neither **His** flesh did see corruption.

Acts 13:35 Wherefore he saith also in another Psalm, "**Thou** shalt not suffer **Thine Holy One** to see corruption".

*Acts 2:33 Therefore being by the right hand of **God**, exalted, and having received of the **Father** the promise of the **Holy Ghost**, **He** hath shed forth this, which ye now see and hear.

Acts 10:45 And they of the circumcision which believed were astonished, as many as came with Peter, because that on the Gentiles also was poured out the gift of the **Holy Ghost.**

*Acts 2:34 For David is not ascended into the Heavens: but he saith himself, "The **LORD** said unto my **Lord**, 'Sit **Thou** on **My** right hand'".

Psalm 110:1 The **LORD** said unto my **Lord**, "Sit **Thou** at **My** right hand, until **I** make **Thine** enemies the footstool".

*Acts 3:22 For Moses truly said unto the fathers, "A **PROPHET** SHALL THE **LORD** YOUR **GOD** RAISE UP UNTO YOU OF YOUR BRETHREN, LIKE UNTO ME: **HIM** SHALL YE HEAR IN ALL THINGS WHATSOEVER **HE** SHALL SAY UNTO YOU.

*Acts 4:11 "This is the **Stone** which was set at nought of you builders, which is become the **Head of the Corner.**

Isaiah 28:16 Therefore thus saith the **LORD God**, "Behold! **I** lay in Zion for a **Foundation**, a **Stone**, a **Tried Stone**, a **Precious Corner Stone**, a **Sure Foundation**: he that believeth shall not make haste".

Matthew 21:42 **Jesus** saith unto them, "Did ye never read in the Scriptures, the **Stone** which the builders rejected, the same is become the **Head** of the **Corner**: This is the **LORD's** doing, and it is marvelous in our eyes?

*Acts 4:25 Who by the mouth of **Thy** servant David hast said, "Why did the heathen rage, and the people imagine vain things?

Psalm 2:1, 2 Why do the heathen rage, and the people imagine a vain thing? The kings of the

Earth set themselves, and the rulers take counsel together, against the **LORD**, and **His Anointed**,

*Acts 7:37 This is that Moses, which said unto the children of Israel, "A **Prophet** shall the **LORD** your **God** raise up unto you of your brethren, like unto **Me**; **Him** shall ye hear".

*Acts 8:32 The place of the Scripture which he read was this, **HE** WAS LED AS A SHEEP TO THE SLAUGHTER; AND LIKE A LAMB DUMB BEFORE HIS SHEARER, SO OPENED **HE** NOT **HIS** MOUTH:

*Acts 13:33 **God** hath fulfilled the same unto us their children, in that **He** hath raised up **Jesus** again; as it is also written in the second Psalm, **Thou** art **My Son**, this day have **I Begotten Thee.**

Psalm 2:7 **I** will declare the decree: The **LORD** hath said unto **Me**, **Thou** art **My Son**; this day have **I Begotten Thee.**

Hebrew 1:5 For unto which of the angels said **He** at any time, "**Thou** art **My Son**, this day have **I Begotten Thee**"? And again, "**I** will be to **Him** a **Father**, and **He** shall be to **Me** a **Son**"?

*Acts 13:34 And as concerning that **He** raised **Him** up from the dead, now no more to return to corruption, **He** said on this wise, "**I** will give **You** the sure mercies of David".

God said....

Isaiah 55:3 Incline your ear, and come unto **Me**: hear, and your soul shall live; and **I** will make an everlasting Covenant with you, even the sure Mercies of David.

*Acts 13:35 Wherefore **He** saith also in another Psalm, "**THOU** SHALT NOT SUFFER **THINE HOLY ONE** TO SEE CORRUPTION".

*Acts 13:47 For so hath the **LORD** commanded us, saying, "**I** have set **Thee** to be a **Light** of the Gentiles, that **Thou** shouldest be for Salvation unto the ends of the Earth".

*Acts 28:26 Saying, "Go unto this people, and say", "Hearing ye shall hear, and shall not understand; and seeing ye shall see, and not perceive:

*Acts 28:28 Be it known therefore unto you, that the Salvation of **God** is sent unto the Gentiles, and that they will hear it.

Isaiah 42:1 Behold! **My Servant**, whom **I** uphold; **Mine Elect**, in whom **My Soul** delighteth; **I** have put **My Spirit** upon **Him**: **He** shall bring forth Judgment to the Gentiles.

*Romans 1:3 Concerning **His Son, Jesus Christ** our **Lord**, which was made of the seed of David, according to the flesh.

*Romans 1:4 And declared to be the **Son** of **God** with Power! According to the **Spirit** of **Holiness**, by the Resurrection from the dead:

Psalm 2:7 I will declare the decree: the **LORD** hath said unto **Me**, **Thou** art **My Son**; this day have **I Begotten Thee**.

Psalm 16:10, 11 For **Thou** wilt not leave **My Soul** in hell; neither wilt **Thou** suffer **Thine Holy One** to see corruption. 11) **Thou** wilt shew **Me** the path of life: in **Thy** presence is fullness of joy; at **Thy** right hand there are pleasures for evermore.

*Romans 5:8 But **God** commendeth **His** love toward us, in that, while we were yet sinners, **Christ** died for us.

Isaiah 53:5 But **He** was wounded for our transgressions, **He** was bruised for our iniquities: the chastisement of our peace was upon **Him**; and with **His** stripes, we are healed.

*Romans 5:18 Therefore as by the offence of one judgment came upon all men to condemnation; even so by the righteousness of **One**, the free gift came upon all men unto justification of life.

*Romans 9:33 As it is written, Behold! **I** lay in Sion a **Stumbling Stone** and **Rock of Offence**: and whosoever believeth on **Him** shall not be ashamed.

*Romans 10:11 For the Scripture saith, whosoever believeth on **Him** shall not be ashamed".

*Romans 10:16 "But they have not all obeyed the Gospel". For Esaias saith, "**Lord**, who hath believed our report?"

*Romans 11:9, 10 And David saith, "LET THEIR TABLE BE MADE A SNARE, AND A TRAP, AND A STUMBLING BLOCK, AND A RECOMPENSE UNTO THEM:

*Romans 15:3 For even **Christ** pleased not **Himself**; but as it is written, "The reproaches of them that reproached **Thee**, fell on **Me**.

Psalm 69:9 For the zeal of **Thine** House hath eaten me up; and the reproaches of them that reproached **Thee** are fallen upon me.

*Romans 15:12 And again, Esaias saith, "There shall be a **Root** of Jesse, and **He** that shall rise to reign over the Gentiles; in **Him** shall the Gentiles trust".

Isaiah 11:10 And in that day there shall be a **Root** of Jesse, which shall stand for an ensign of the people to it shall the Gentiles seek: and in **His** rest shall be glorious.

God said....

*1 Corinthians 15:3 For I delivered unto you first of all that which I also received, how that **Christ** died for our sins according to the Scriptures; And that **He** was buried, and that **He** rose again the third day according to the Scriptures.

*2 Corinthians 5:21 For **He** hath made **Him** *to be sin for us, who knew no sin; that we might be made the Righteousness* of **God** in **Him**.

Isaiah 53:6, 9 All we like sheep have gone astray; we have turned everyone to his own way; and the **LORD** hath laid on **Him** the iniquity of us all. 9) And **He** made **His** grave with the wicked, and with the rich in **His** death; because **He** had done no violence, neither was any deceit in **His** mouth.

*2 Corinthians 6:2 (For **He** saith, "I have heard **Thee** in a time accepted, and in the day of *Salvation*, have **I** succoured **Thee**: Behold! now is the day of Salvation).

Isaiah 49:8 Thus saith the **LORD**, In an acceptable time have **I** heard **Thee**, and in the day of Salvation, have **I** helped **Thee**: And **I** will preserve **Thee**, and give **Thee** a Covenant of the people to establish the Earth, to cause to inherit the desolate heritages.

*Galatians 2:20 I am crucified with **Christ**: nevertheless, I live; yet not I, but **Christ** liveth in me: and the life which I now live in the flesh I live by the faith of the **Son** of **God**, *who* loved me, and gave **Himself** for me.

Isaiah 53:12 Therefore will **I** divide **Him** a portion with the great, and **He** shall divide the spoil with the strong; because **He** hath poured out **His** **Soul** into death: and **He** was numbered with the transgressors; and **He** bare the sin of many and made intercession for the transgressors.

*Galatians 3:8 And the Scripture, forseeing that **God** would justify the heathen through faith, preached before the gospel unto Abraham, saying, "In thee shall all nations be blessed".

*Galatians 3:16 Now to Abraham and his **Seed**, were promises made. **He** saith not, "And to seeds of many; but as of one", "And to thy **Seed**, which is **Christ**".

*Galatians 4:4 But when the fullness of the time was come, **God** sent forth **His Son**, made of a woman, under the law.

Isaiah 7:14 Therefore, The **LORD Himself**, shall give you a sign; Behold, a virgin shall conceive, and bear a **Son**, and shall call **His** Name **Immanuel**.

*Ephesians 2:14 For **He** is our peace, who hath made both one, and hath broken down the middle wall of partition between us.

Isaiah 9:6 For unto us a **Child** is born, unto us a **Son** is given: and the Government shall be upon **His** shoulder: and **His** Name shall be called **Wonderful**, **Counsellor**, The **Mighty God**, the **Everlasting Father**, the **Prince** of **Peace**.

Micah 5:5 And this **Man** shall be the **Peace** when the Assyrian shall come into our land: and when he shall tread in our palaces, then shall we raise against him seven shepherds, and eight principal men.

*Ephesians 4:8 Wherefore **He** saith, "When **He** ascended up on high, **He** led captivity captive, and gave gifts unto men.

Psalm 68:18 **Thou** hast ascended on High, **Thou** hast led captivity captive: **Thou** hast received gifts for men; yea for the rebellious also that the **LORD God** might dwell among them.

Colossians 2:15 And having spoiled principalities and powers, **He** made a shew of them openly, triumphing over them in it.

*Ephesians 5:14 Wherefore **He** saith, "Awake thou that sleepest, and arise from the dead, and **Christ** shall give thee light.

God said....

Isaiah 26:19 Thy dead men shall live! together with my dead body, shall they arise! Awake! And sing! Ye that dwell in dust: for thy dew is as the dew of herbs, and the Earth shall cast out the dead.

Isaiah 60:1 Arise! Shine: For is thy light has come! And the glory of the **LORD** is risen upon thee.

*Philippians 2:9 Wherefore **God** also hath highly exalted **Him** and given **Him** a Name which is above every Name:

*1 Timothy 1:15 This is a faithful saying, and worthy of all acceptations, that **Christ Jesus** came into the world to save sinners; of whom I am chief.

*2 Timothy 2:11 It is a faithful saying: For if we be dead with **Him**, we shall also live with **Him**.

TIMELINE: 70 A.D.

*Hebrews 1:3 Who being the brightness of **His** glory, and the express image of **His** person, and upholding all things by the Word of **His** power. When **He** had by **Himself** purged our sins, sat down on the right hand of the **Majesty** on high.

John 1:14 And the **Word** was made flesh, and dwelt among us, (And we beheld **His** Glory, the Glory as of the **Only Begotten** of the **Father**), full of Grace and Truth.

Hebrews 7:27 Who needeth not daily, as those high priests, to offer up sacrifice, first for his own sins, and then for the people's: for this **He** did once, when **He** offered up **Himself**.

*Hebrews 1:5, 6 For unto which of the angels said **He** at any time, **THOU ARE MY SON**, THIS DAY HAVE **I BEGOTTEN THEE**? 6) And again, when **He** bringeth in the **First Begotten**, into the world **He** saith, "AND LET ALL THE ANGELS OF **GOD** WORSHIP **HIM**.

*Hebrews 1:8 But unto the **Son**, **He** saith, **THY** THRONE, O **GOD**, IS FOR EVER AND EVER: A SCEPTRE OF RIGHTEOUSNESS IS THE SCEPTRE OF **THY** KINGDOM.

*Hebrews 1:10 And, **Thou**, **LORD**, in the beginning hast laid the foundation of the Earth; and the Heavens are the works of **Thine** hands:

John 1:3 All things were made by **Him**; and without **Him** was not anything made that was made.

God said....

*Hebrews 1:13 But to which of the angels said **He** at any time, "Sit on **My** right hand, until **I** make **Thine** enemies **Thy** footstool?

Psalm 110:1 The **LORD** said unto **My Lord**, "Sit **Thou** at **My** right hand, until I make **Thine** enemies **Thy** footstool.

*Hebrews 2:12 Saying, I will declare **Thy** Name unto **My** brethren, in the midst of the church will I sing praise unto **Thee**.

*Hebrews 2:13 And again, **I** will put **My** trust in **Him**. And again, Behold! **I** and the children which **God** hath given **Me**.

Isaiah 8:17, 18 And I will wait upon the **LORD**, that hideth **His** face from the House of Jacob, and I will look for **Him**. 18) Behold, I and the children whom the **LORD** hath given me are for signs and wonders in Israel from the **LORD** of Hosts, which dwelleth in mount Zion.

*Hebrews 5:5, 6 So also **Christ** glorified not **Himself** to be made an **High Priest**; but **He** that said unto **Him**, Thou art **My Son**, today have **I Begotten Thee**. 6) As **He** saith also in another place, **THOU** ART A **PRIEST** FOR EVER, AFTER THE ORDER OF MELCHISEDEC.

*Hebrews 7:14 For it is evident that our **Lord** sprang out of Judah; of which tribe Moses spake nothing concerning priesthood.

Isaiah 11:1 And there shall come forth a **Rod** out of the stem of Jesse, and a **Branch** shall grow out of his roots:

*Hebrews 7:17 For **He** testifieth, **THOU** ART A **PRIEST** FOR EVER AFTER THE ORDER OF MELCHISEDEC.

Psalm 110:4 The **Lord** hath sworn, and will not repent, **THOU** ART A PRIEST FOR EVER AFTER THE ORDER OF MELCHIZEDEK.

*Hebrews 7:21 (For those priests were made without an oath; but this with an oath by **Him** that said unto **Him**, "The **Lord** sware and will not repent, **THOU** ART A PRIEST FOR EVER AFTER THE ORDER OF MELCHISEDEC):

*Hebrews 8:8 For finding fault with them, **He** saith, "BEHOLD! THE DAYS COME, SAITH THE **LORD**, WHEN **I** WILL MAKE A NEW COVENANT WITH THE HOUSE OF ISRAEL AND WITH THE HOUSE OF JUDAH"

*Hebrews 10:5 Wherefore, when **He** cometh into the world, **He** saith, "SACRIFICE AND OFFERING, **THOU** WOULDEST NOT, BUT A BODY HAST THOU PREPARED ME"

*Hebrews 10:12, 13 But this **Man**, after **He** had offered one sacrifice for sins forever, sat down on the right hand of **God**, 13) From henceforth expecting till **His** enemies be made **His** footstool.

*Hebrews 10:16 "THIS IS THE COVENANT THAT **I** WILL MAKE WITH THEM AFTER THOSE DAYS",

SAITH THE **LORD**, **I** WILL PUT **MY** LAWS INTO THEIR HEARTS, AND IN THEIR MINDS, WILL **I** WRITE THEM.

Jeremiah 31:33 "But this shall be the Covenant that **I** will make with the House of Israel"; "After those days", saith the **LORD**, "**I** will put **My** law in their inward parts and write it in their hearts; and will be their **God**, and they shall be **My** people.

*Hebrews 10:17 "AND THEIR SINS AND INIQUITIES WILL **I** REMEMBER NO MORE".

Jeremiah 31:34 And they shall teach no more every man his neighbor, and every man his brother, saying, 'Know the **LORD**': for they shall all know **Me**, from the least of them unto the greatest of them, saith the **LORD**: for **I** will forgive their iniquity, and **I** will remember their sin no more".

God said....

*1 Peter 1:2 Elect, according to the foreknowledge of **God** the **Father**, through sanctification of the **Spirit**, unto obedience and sprinkling of the blood of **Jesus Christ**: Grace unto you, and peace be multiplied.

Isaiah 52:15 So shall **He** sprinkle many nations; the kings shall shut their mouths at **Him**: for that which had not been told them shall they see; and that which they had not heard shall they consider.

*1 Peter 1:19 But with the precious blood of **Christ**, as a lamb without blemish and without spot, made you overseers, to feed the church of **God**, which **He** hath purchased with **His** own blood.

Acts 20:28 Take heed therefore unto yourselves, and to all the flock, over which the **Holy Ghost** hath made you overseers, to feed the church of **God** which **He** hath purchased with **His** own blood.

Exodus 12:5 Your lamb shall be without blemish, a make of the first year: ye shall take it out from the sheep, or from the goats:

*1 Peter 2:6 Wherefore also it is contained in the Scripture, Behold! **I** lay in Sion a **Chief Corner Stone; Elect, Precious**: and he that believeth on **Him**, shall not be confounded.

Isaiah 28:16 Therefore thus saith the **LORD God**, Behold! **I** lay in Zion for a foundation a **Stone**, a **Tried Stone**, a **Precious Corner Stone**, **a Sure Foundation**: he that believeth shall not make haste.

*1 Peter 2:7 Unto you therefore which believe **He** is precious: but unto them which be disobedient, the **Stone** which the builders disallowed, the same is made the **Head** of the **Corner**.

Matthew 16:18 "And **I** say also unto thee, that thou art Peter, and upon this rock will **I** build **My** *Church*; and the gates of hell shall not prevail against it".

Matthew 21:42 **Jesus** saith unto them, "Did ye never read in the Scriptures? The **Stone** which the builders rejected, the same is become the **Head** of the **Corner**: this is the **LORD's** doing, and it is marvelous in our eyes".

Psalm 118:22 The **Stone** which the builders refused is become the **Head Stone** of the **Corner**.

*1 Peter 2:8 And a **Stone of Stumbling**, and a **Rock of Offence**, even to them which stumble at the **Word**, being disobedient: whereunto also they were appointed.

Isaiah 8:14 And **He** shall be for a **Sanctuary**, but for a **Stone of Stumbling** and for a **Rock of Offence** to both the Houses of Israel, for a gin and for a snare to the inhabitants of Jerusalem.

*1 Peter 2:22 **Who** did no sin, neither was guile found in **His** mouth:

Isaiah 53:9 And **He** made **His** grave with the wicked, and with the rich, in **His** death; because **He** had done no violence, neither was any deceit in **His** mouth.

*1 Peter 2:23 **Who**, when **He** was reviled, reviled not again; when **He** suffered, **He** threatened not; but committed **Himself** to **Him** that judgeth righteously:

*1 Peter 2:24 **Who His** own self bare our sins in **His** own body, on the tree, that we, being dead to sins, should live unto Righteousness: by **Whose** stripes ye were healed.

Isaiah 53:5 But **He** was wounded for our transgressions, **He** was bruised for our iniquities: the chastisement of our peace was upon **Him**: and with **His** stripes we are healed.

*1 Peter 2:25 For ye were as sheep going astray; but are now returned unto the **Shepherd** and **Bishop** of your souls.

God said....

*Revelation 3:7 To the angel of the church in Philadelphia write, these things saith **He** that is **Holy**, **He** that is **True**, **He** that hath the Key of David, **He** that openeth, and no man shutteth; and shutteth, and no man openeth".

*Revelation 5:12 Saying with a loud voice, "Worthy is the **Lamb** that was slain to receive Power and Riches, and Wisdom, and Strength, and Honour, and Glory, and Blessing".

Isaiah 53:7 **He** was oppressed, and **He** was afflicted, yet **He** opened not **His** mouth: **He** is brought as a lamb to the slaughter, and as a sheep before her shearers is dumb, so **He** openeth not **His** mouth.

Amen and Amen

Printed in the United States
by Baker & Taylor Publisher Services